TYPING

THE EASY WAY

Second Edition

WARREN T. SCHIMMEL

PRESIDENT
THE BERKELEY SCHOOL
WHITE PLAINS, N.Y.

AND

STANLEY A. LIEBERMAN

BUSINESS EDUCATION CONSULTANT
NEW YORK, N.Y.

BARRON'S

BARRON'S EDUCATIONAL SERIES, INC.
New York • London • Toronto • Sydney

All inquiries should be addressed to:
Barron's Educational Series, Inc.
250 Wireless Boulevard
Hauppauge, New York 11788

Library of Congress Catalog Card No. 88-8614
International Standard Book No. 0-8120-4080-5

Library of Congress Cataloging-in-Publication Data

Schimmel, Warren T.
    Typing the easy way / Warren T. Schimmel and Stanley A. Lieberman.
    — 2nd ed.
        p.   cm.
    Includes index.
    ISBN 0-8120-4080-5
    1. Typewriting.   I. Lieberman, Stanley A.   II. Title.
Z49.S38 1988
652.3'024 — dc19   88-8614
                                                     CIP

PRINTED IN THE UNITED STATES OF AMERICA

01   100   9876

CONTENTS

NOTES

Worksheets 1-5 follow page ***66***

INTRODUCTION

In this book you will learn to type with speed, with accuracy, and with rhythm. By Lesson 57, you should be typing at 45 wpm, a speed which will prepare you to enter the typing job market where typing skill is required, should you so desire.

In the first part of the book you will learn the keyboard. From then on, you will be taught how to apply this new skill to various situations encountered in everyday life: typing memos, bills, tabulations, letters, envelopes, reports, forms, resumes. Helpful tips are given on word division, proofreading, composing at the typewriter, and correcting techniques. We suggest that you try to practice every day, spending approximately 30 to 45 minutes per day on the average lesson. The more you practice, the more your skill and speed will increase. Timed writings and progress charts are included so that you can measure your progress. From here on, it's up to you—so go to it!

Learning the Parts of Your Typewriter

To begin, you must become familiar with the various parts of your typewriter. Although letter positions remain the same on all machines, some symbols and punctuation mark locations differ. Illustrations are provided of two basic machine types: the main parts of each are noted. Take a minute to study the diagrams that follow, and compare with your typewriter.

Now you are ready to insert your paper:

1. Set the PAPER GUIDE at 0 (this will be true for most typing jobs).

2. Pull the PAPER BAIL forward or up (depending upon your machine). To insert the paper, place it behind the CYLINDER with the left edge against the paper guide, and, with your right hand on the RIGHT CYLINDER KNOB, roll the paper into position for typing. Now, press the CARRIAGE RELEASE on either the left or right side of the typewriter and move the carriage freely back and forth. Then check the top of the paper with the ALIGNMENT SCALE; if it is not even, press the PAPER RELEASE and adjust the paper. Practice removing the paper by using the paper release with your right hand and pulling the paper gently with your left.

3. Set the LINE-SPACE REGULATOR at 1 for single spacing, 2 for double spacing, or 3 for triple spacing. (The VARIABLE LINE-SPACER—or the LINE-FINDER or RATCHET RELEASE—allows you to type above or below the original typing line. This is useful in making corrections, typing superior numerals, or filling in forms.)

4. Practice using the CARRIAGE RETURN (a key on electrics, a lever on manuals). On electrics you activate the carriage return key with the right little finger; on manuals you throw the carriage with the left hand against the return lever.

5. To set the margins, procedures vary for different typewriters. On some machines you adjust margins by hand without the use of a set key; each stop is set separately by pressing down on top of the MARGIN STOP, sliding it left or right to the desired point on the scale, and then releasing the stop. On machines with spring-set margin stops or levers (sometimes called "Magic Margins"), first press the left MARGIN SET KEY, move the carriage to the desired point on the scale, and release the key. Now do the same with the right key. Some electrics have margin set keys on the keyboard; here you would first move the carriage to the left margin, press down the margin set key, move the carriage to the desired point, and then release the key, repeating the sequence for the right margin. The MARGIN RELEASE KEY will release the margin on the right side so that you can type beyond the margin if necessary to finish a word.

6. The BACKSPACE KEY moves the element or carriage back one space. On electric typewriters it is a repeating key if pressed firmly.

Note: At this point, it may be good to mention the difference between pica and elite type machines. Pica (large) type prints 10 characters to an inch; elite (small) type, 12 characters to an inch. On standard typing paper, which is 8½ inches wide, a pica machine can type 85 characters (10 × 8½), with 42 the center point, whereas an elite machine will type 102 characters (12 × 8½), with 51 the center point.

In the following lessons, you will note directions telling you to set margins for a line of 40 spaces, 45 spaces, 50 spaces, etc. Just remember that one half the spaces must be to the left of the center point of your typewriter and the other half are to the right of the center point. For example, margins for a 40-space line on an elite machine would be 31 and 71 (51 = center point; ½ of 40 = 20; 51 − 20 = 31). On a pica machine, the margins for a 40-space line are 22 and 62 (42 = center point; ½ of 40 = 20; 42 − 20 = 22). Setting margins is covered in detail in LESSON 22.

Practicing Correct Posture

Before you begin to type, you must be sure that both your HAND POSITION and BODY POSTURE are correct and comfortable:

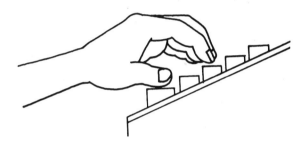

1. Place curved fingers lightly on the "home" keys ASDF JKL;. The right thumb should rest lightly on the space bar of a manual typewriter but not touch the space bar of an electric machine (which would automatically repeat). Bend your hands slightly at the wrist, keeping palms off the typewriter frame. On electric typewriters, you must not rest your fingers on the home keys, but just above them. (Make believe that the keys are too hot to touch!) In typing, if you have a manual typewriter, you must use a very sharp "stinging" stroke. On an electric machine, remember to "tap" the keys very lightly; otherwise, the key will repeat.

2. Your chair should be placed so that your arms reach out, elbows loosely at your sides. Sit erect but relaxed, with your body in front of the "H" key, about a hand's width (4 to 5 inches) from the frame of the typewriter. Both feet should be flat on the floor, one foot a few inches ahead of the other, about 6 to 8 inches apart for balance.

REMEMBER: FEET FLAT / FINGERS CURVED / PALMS OFF FRAME

Determining Your Typing Speed

Figure your typing speed by determining how many "words" you typed in the time allowed: Every 5 strokes (including spaces) is considered a "standard" *word.* For example, if you typed a 50-stroke line in 1 minute, you have typed 10 words a minute (50 strokes divided by the standard 5-stroke word). If you typed a complete 50-stroke line and an additional 15 strokes (3 standard words) in the minute allowed, you would have typed 13 words a minute. If the length of the timing is more than 1 minute, you would divide the total number of words by the time allowed (20 words in 2 minutes equals 10 words per minute, or 10 wpm, the abbreviation we will use in the book).

In any timing, your goal should be to have no more errors than the number of minutes you type. Thus, if you type for 1 minute, there should be no more than 1 error. If your typing is perfect, so much the better!

In the timed writings in this book, the number of cumulative standard words is shown at the end of each line of writing.

Typing Rhythm

The idea of typing rhythm is important. You should strive for an even, unhurried, smooth touch. Rhythmic typing rests your fingers and arms; uneven, hurried attacks result from and increase tenseness in your hands or arms. Spurting may win a footrace, but typing in spurts is bound to cause fatigue, tension, and errors, and will slow down your speed.

Use your inherent sense of rhythm when you practice typing. If you have a manual typewriter, watch the carriage to see if it is moving smoothly without stops and starts. Are you stroking each key with the same pressure and at a steady pace?

Acknowledgment

We are indebted to our editor, Pamella M. Wheeler, for her many constructive suggestions and skillful, professional work.

INDEX

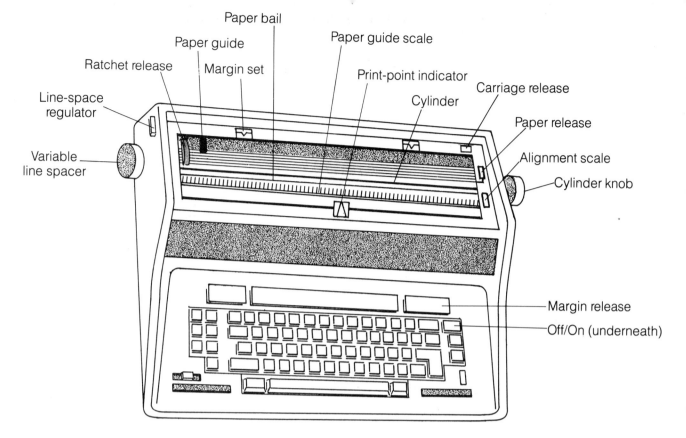

Electric typewriter

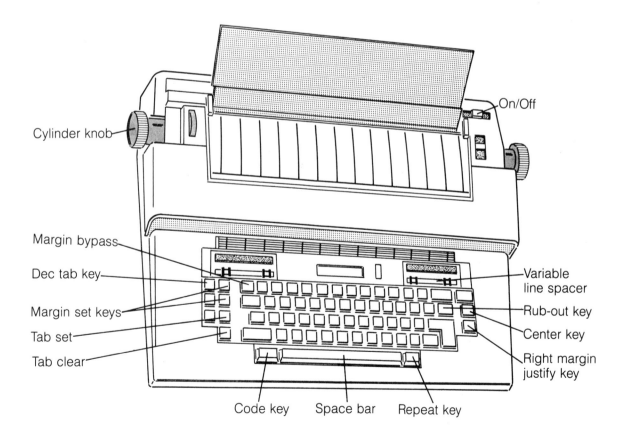

Electronic typewriter

INDEX

CHART YOUR PROGRESS

Timed Practice *or* Skill Improvement Exercise in Lesson	GOAL	Speed per Minute (WPM)	Number of Errors per Minute	Timed Practice *or* Skill Improvement Exercise in Lesson	GOAL	Speed per Minute (WPM)	Number of Errors per Minute
5	10			33	33		
6	10			34	34		
7	11			35	35		
8	11			36	36		
9	12			37	37		
10	12			38	38		
11	13			39	39		
12	13			40	40		
13	14			41	40		
14	14			42	40		
15	15			43	41		
16	16			44	41		
17	17			45	41		
18	18			46	42		
19	19			47	42		
20	20			48	42		
21	21			49	43		
22	22			50	43		
23	23			51	43		
24	24			52	43		
25	25			53	44		
26	26			54	44		
27	27			55	44		
28	28			56	44		
29	29			57	45		
30	30			58	45		
31	31			59	45		
32	32			60	45		

EXTENDED TIMED WRITINGS CHART

TIMING NO.	DATE	3-MINUTE TIMING (WPM)	NUMBER OF ERRORS	5-MINUTE TIMING (WPM)	NUMBER OF ERRORS
1					

CHAPTER

1

LEARNING
THE
TYPEWRITER
KEYBOARD

TIMING 9

	TOTAL WORDS
Most countries in the world have now changed to the Metric	14
system. This is a system of decimal measurement that is both	27
practical and efficient. It was originally proposed by a reli-	41
gious person in France in the late 1600's, but it would take a	54
century for the French to officially adopt the system in 1840.	67
By the turn of this century, there were many countries that did	81
the same.	83
The most recent countries to make the change were some of	97
the most rigid holdouts. England, Australia, and Canada--all of	111
these have now adopted the metric system, thus making the United	125
States the last of two countries to convert. America had planned	139
to convert in the 1970's; for one reason or another total conver-	153
sion just never took place. Most adults felt that it was too dif-	167
ficult to learn and basically were just too lazy to try.	179
There are many who think that one has to convert everything	193
to the old system to learn to work in metric. That is not true.	207
Actually, nothing could be farther from the truth. The best way	221
to grasp metric is simply to work within it. Don't convert!	234
Forget the old! Think metric! After a while you will find it a	248
very easy system to use, and you will easily see and understand	262
how each part is related to the other. Eventually the need to	275
convert will vanish.	279
In the United States many industries have begun to use the	293
metric system. These are usually companies involved in interna-	307
tional trade and companies who wish to compete successfully. At	321
least we are beginning to use it even if slowly at best. With	335
just a little bit of additional effort, we can set a new goal	348
for total conversion by the early 1990s.	357

TIMING 10

	TOTAL WORDS
What has happened to the service we used to get in business?	14
When one drove into a gas station, the attendant automatically	28
washed the windows of the car and pulled up the lid of the hood	42
to see if we needed oil. Now they just give gas and that happens	56
if we don't serve ourselves. On the bus, the driver used to call	70
out the names of the streets. If the vehicle was crowded, we al-	84
ways knew where we were on our trip. Today we have to fend for	98
ourselves.	100
Perhaps this has developed because we as consumers have gotten	114
used to being self-servers. The supermarket is the best example.	128
The department store is another. This led to a decrease in the	142
services that business felt it had to give. Perhaps we have come	156
too far towards the extreme. If you need help in a store nowadays,	170
it is quite possible that you will have to search and search for	184
someone to wait on you or to answer your questions accurately.	197
Sales help used to be polite and efficient. They used polite	211
words and were knowledgeable of their merchandise. This is not	224
so today. Many times the sales help is satisfied to say that they	238
don't know and simply walk on their way. It is the customer who	252
may have to say "thank you" to the clerk before the worker gets	266
the hint.	268
Is the pace of our life so rapid today that we have forgotten	282
that good service is essential to all parties in a business opera-	296
tion? Have we taken it all for granted too long now to effect an	310
improvement? Certainly not. It is the duty of the businessman to	324
give good service, and it is the duty of the consumer to demand it.	338

LESSON 1

OBJECTIVE: To learn the home row keys and to use the space bar.

NOTE: Small l is used as number 1 on some typewriters. (See pages 13 and 16)

DIRECTIONS: Place fingers on the home row keys of asdf jkl;. Type each line 3 times, spacing once after each set of letters as shown. To space, tap the space bar with the right thumb. Double-space (return carriage twice) after each typed group of 3 lines. Your goal should be to type each line of Problem 1-1 without an error before going on to Problem 1-2.

MARGINS: 40-space line
SINGLE SPACING

DIRECTIONS: Place fingers on the home row keys. Type each line 3 times, spacing once after each set of letters as shown. Double-space after each group of 3 lines. Your goal should be to type each line of Problem 1-2 without an error before going on to LESSON 2.

MARGINS: 40-space line
SINGLE SPACING

REMEMBER that on most electric typewriters holding the space bar down will permit the typewriter to continue spacing.

THE HOME ROW KEYS A S D F J K L ;

Before you begin this lesson, be sure you have carefully read the Introduction to this book.

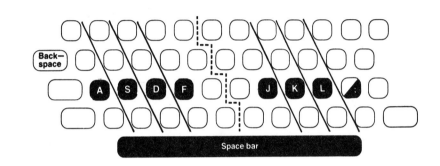

1-1 THE HOME ROW

```
fff jjj fff jjj fj fj fff jjj ff jj f j
ddd kkk ddd kkk dk dk ddd kkk dd kk d k
sss lll sss lll sl sl sss lll ss ll s l
aaa ;;; aaa ;;; a; a; aaa ;;; aa ;; a ;
aaa sss kkk ask dad aaa ddd dad ask dad
```

1-2 ADDED PRACTICE

```
sss aaa ddd sad dad lll aaa ddd lad lad
fff aaa ddd fad lll aaa ddd lad fad sad
a;a sls dkd fjf fjf dkd sls a;a a lass;
ask sad lad fad dad lad sad dad ask lad
```

TIMING 7

Self-confidence is a matter of mindset. It comes from a nur-	14
tured belief in oneself and starts at an early age. We must	27
understand that we will never be able to perform each task in our	41
life perfectly, but it is better to try to perform them rather	55
than not.	57
Sometimes we have to push ourselves to learn to like ourselves.	71
So often it is easy to put ourselves down when we don't accomplish	85
what we set out to do or we don't do something as well as someone	99
else. Usually we are at the mercy of ourselves before we are at	113
the mercy of others.	118
Everyone has potential. Everyone has the ability to learn.	132
In some tasks it takes practice, practice, and more practice. One	146
attempt may not be enough. Even several attempts may be insuf-	160
ficient. Regardless, that is no reason to quit. If the task or	174
endeavor is something we want to do and like to do, then we should	188
keep on trying. Even if we consider that there may be some very	202
real limitations, we shouldn't let any of these keep us from at	216
least making an attempt.	221
People like different things and do them better than others.	235
Each person can do something well. There are many, for example,	249
who think they could never become an artist; but if they start at	263
the beginning of the skill-building process and continue to work	277
on the skill that is needed to make good art, they can succeed.	291
There will always be stumbling blocks to what we do or want to do.	305
Sometimes we have to take detours or consider alternate routes.	319
What is important is to set those goals and keep going after them.	333

| 1 | 2 | 3 | 4 | 5 | 6 | 7 | 8 | 9 | 10 | 11 | 12 | 13 | 14 | TOTAL WORDS

TIMING 8

| 1 | 2 | 3 | 4 | 5 | 6 | 7 | 8 | 9 | 10 | 11 | 12 | 13 | 14 | TOTAL WORDS

For the past four decades people have been moving away from	14
cities and living in the suburbs. A greater number than ever be-	28
fore are even now working in the suburbs especially in what are	42
called "outtowns" located near interchanges of superhighways.	55
Families moved to the suburbs for many reasons. First, of	69
course, they wanted more space to build larger homes. They	82
wanted lots of open air areas where they could spread out their	95
schools and spread out their parks. This also included the spread-	109
out spaces for the development of the shopping mall, which is the	123
stamp of many a suburb.	128
Then, all of a sudden people were finding themselves moved	141
too far out as each new generation wanted its own larger space.	154
This new generation also discovered something else--the city.	167
Because of them, many young people are returning to the city and	181
taking part in its redevelopment.	188
The city offers tremendous advantages. First of all it has	202
energy and excitement already built in. It usually has an effi-	216
cient transportation system dating from the "old days" that makes	230
it easy to get from one place to another without having to use an	244
automobile. The city is rich in architecture and in history--	257
something that those who moved to the suburbs forgot or never	270
knew. There are theaters, museums, stores, etc., that have been	283
established for many years. Even the city park is an interesting	297
phenomenon to behold especially on a Sunday.	306
Yes, the city is certainly coming back into its own. Its	319
rebirth of richness and vitality will again make it a viable	332
choice for both working and living.	340

| 1 | 2 | 3 | 4 | 5 | 6 | 7 | 8 | 9 | 10 | 11 | 12 | 13 | 14 | TOTAL WORDS

LESSON 2

REACH— THEN RETURN TO THE HOME KEYS.

NEW KEYS
R T U Y

OBJECTIVE: To review the letters previously learned and to learn 4 new keys.

DIRECTIONS: Place fingers on the home row keys of asdf·jkl;. Type each of the following lines 3 times, double-spacing between each group of 3 lines.

MARGINS: 40-space line
SINGLE SPACING

2-1 REVIEW

```
aaa ;;; sss lll ddd kkk fff jjj aaa ;;;
ask lad dad fad ask asks lads dads lass
```

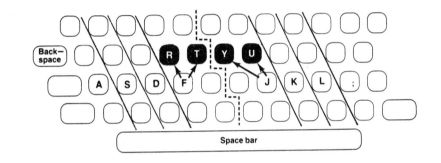

2-2 NEW REACHES

```
R Key:  fff frf rrr frf frf rrr fff frf rrr frf
T Key:  fff ftf ttt fff ftf ttt fff ftf ttt ftf
U Key:  jjj juj uuu jjj juj uuu jjj juj uuu juj
Y Key:  jjj jyj yyy jjj jyj yyy jjj jyj yyy jyj
```

REMEMBER: *While you are learning the keyboard, it is good practice not to go on to the next problem or lesson until you can type without error each line you are studying.*

2-3 USING THE NEW KEYS

```
rrr far far rrr rat rat fr fr frff rrr;
ttt fat fat ttt tar tar ft ft ftff ttt;
uuu rut rut uuu jut jut ju ju jujj uuu;
yyy jury jury yyy jyj yard yard jyj jyy
```

2-4 ADDED PRACTICE

```
ask ask just just lad lad fry fry fasts
fur fur last last dull dull darts darts
duty duty fast fast rust rust dark dark
say; say; data data dust dust jars jars
```

SPACE *once after a semicolon.*

TIMING 5

Many companies in America today are experimenting with the four- **14**
day workweek. They are interested in seeing whether or not their em- **28**
ployees are more productive, more willing and eager to do their work, **42**
and whether or not the high absenteeism rate can be cut. So far, the **56**
results have been good; and it appears that by the time we reach the **70**
end of the present century, many firms will be using the four-day work- **84**
week. **85**

One of the advantages of a shorter workweek is that people have **99**
more leisure time to improve the quality of their personal lives. Al- **113**
though many do realize that with more time to be free they can experi- **127**
ment with new hobbies and spend more time with their families, there **141**
is the problem of too much leisure. Some younger people are using **155**
this extra time to get second jobs, which in turn defeats the original **169**
reason for their extra leisure and causes reverse results on their **183**
primary job. **186**

How are these companies experimenting? Well, the first way is to **200**
have the employees put in more hours per day so that in fact they are **214**
working the same number of hours per week. The most efficient plan **228**
seems to have workers complete ten hours per day. Many employees **242**
don't feel that the extra two hours is an imposition and agree that **256**
the advantages far outweigh the disadvantages. The most popular days **270**
to be "off" are Friday and Monday. **277**

Another plan is to continue working the same number of hours per **291**
day and just drop off the extra day. This is being done in companies **305**
where advanced technology is used to complete tasks in less and less **319**
time. **320**

What do you think of the four-day workweek? Do you think you **334**
would use your extra time to realize a better quality of existence? **348**

TIMING 6

The technology of communication is changing rapidly. The ef- **14**
fect that this has had on our world is that it is making it much **28**
smaller. We hear more and more about the term, "Global Village." **42**
It is possible to know in a flash what is happening around the **56**
world. Our television screens show us daily news in the making. **70**
We are there when the event occurs and we see it taking place **83**
right before our eyes. An event in the Middle East or an event in **97**
Asia--even though they are eight or twelve time zones away--can be **111**
seen by us in North America almost instantly. **121**

The computer has added to the speed with which we gather and **135**
transmit information. These, along with satellites that circle **149**
the globe, make us aware that all peoples are really one and that **163**
each nation is intertwined one with the others. This interdepen- **177**
dence is political, economic, and social. An event taking place **191**
in one location can have a profound effect on an event taking **204**
place in another. **208**

Travel has also improved. We now have airplanes that fly at **222**
the speed of sound. They can get us from one continent to another **236**
in a matter of a few hours. The future for air travel looks even **250**
brighter. One day soon we will have airplanes that go into orbit **264**
around the earth. Thus, a trip from New York to Tokyo, which **277**
presently takes about twelve hours, will take only two. **289**

What does all this mean for Man? All people on this planet **303**
are going to have to change their thinking from nationalistic **317**
orientations to international orientations. We will need zest and **331**
zeal to develop new ideas concerning the ways we relate to each **345**
other. The future looks bright and hopeful for Man's ability to **367**
attain global peace and understanding.

LESSON 3

OBJECTIVE: To review the letters previously learned and to learn 4 new keys.

DIRECTIONS: Place fingers on the home row keys. Type each of the following lines 3 times, double-spacing between each set of 3 lines.

MARGINS: 40-space line
SINGLE SPACING

ARMS AND HANDS RELAXED

NEW KEYS
E I G H

3-1 REVIEW

```
ask lad fry jut tar jar jj ff dd kk sss
aa ;; sad salt dull fall dark dust frff
juj jy dad rut yard jury duty say lass;
```

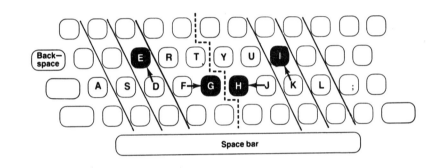

3-2 NEW REACHES

E Key: ddd ded eee ddd ded eee ddd ded eee ded
I Key: kkk kik iii kkk kik iii kkk kik iii kkk
G Key: fff fgf ggg fff fgf ggg fff fgf ggg fff
H Key: jjj jhj hhh jjj jhj hhh jjj jhj hhh jjj

3-3 USING THE NEW KEYS

```
did did lag lag elk elk gas gas hid hid
red red rug tug yes yes age age let let
rug; rug; kiss kiss jilt jilt hale hale
fee; fee; rake rake that that said said
```

3-4 ADDED PRACTICE

```
the tug lad red did; she hid the lists;
let sail; us set the hear high hill is;
did age; the rug hair red; he is; hair;
ask her; side rails; the dig a rut; age
```

TIMING 3

Most people today below the age of forty do not remember the fun   14
of streetcars. There are very few cities left in the world today where   28
the streetcar remains. It became a victim of progress and of the need   42
to make city streets less congested. Was it a mistake to remove it in   56
favor of the bus?   60

Unlikely as it may seem, the streetcar may make a comeback in our   74
urban lives. Because of the expense of building underground railways,   88
many city planners have begun to look at the feasibility of bringing   102
back the streetcar. For one thing, streetcars run on electricity and   116
hence save money in these energy-conscious days. For another, the   130
life of a streetcar is about twenty or thirty years as opposed to a   144
much shorter life for the bus. The ride is smoother and more comfort-   158
able. There are less mechanical problems.   167

In the old days the "trolleys" came in many varieties. For ex-   181
ample, in the summertime there were open-air trolleys. There were   195
high-speed interurban systems that were quite efficient even by today's   209
standards. Children and grownups alike were amused and delighted for   223
decades to hear the clanging bell of the trolley as it stopped to dis-   237
charge or pick up passengers. Then there was the experience of putting   251
a penny on the rail to see it flattened by the trolley as it passed.   265
It was also fun to see the motorman put the trolley pole back on the   279
overhead line after passing a switch.   287

Given a special right-of-way along the side lanes of our streets,   301
the streetcar again has much promise. Such lightweight transit, as   315
it is called, may be a significant answer to the future needs of our   329
transportation system.   334

| 1 | 2 | 3 | 4 | 5 | 6 | 7 | 8 | 9 | 10 | 11 | 12 | 13 | 14 | TOTAL WORDS

TIMING 4

| 1 | 2 | 3 | 4 | 5 | 6 | 7 | 8 | 9 | 10 | 11 | 12 | 13 | 14 | TOTAL WORDS

Travel is one of the best ways to broaden one's horizons. It can   14
be most exciting to visit different countries and learn about different   28
cultures. Not only does one have the opportunity to see differences in   42
the landscapes, but one has a chance to study the different kinds of   56
architecture, meet varied and interesting people, and make comparisons   70
of different kinds of life-styles.   77

In Europe, for example, the variety of and differences between the   91
countries and even cities within the same country can be extraordinary.   105
From the big cities of London, Paris, and Rome, to the farmlands, to   119
the vacation resorts, and to the mountains, you will have the experi-   133
ence of a lifetime.   137

You will enjoy the museums. You will be enthralled by the art   151
and interested in the history. You will enjoy the marvelous churches.   165
You will be fascinated by the quaint inns and taverns as well as with   179
the cafes and the open markets.   186

There are many ways to travel in Europe. Many people rent auto-   200
mobiles because they feel they can have direct control over the routes   214
they choose and the destinations they reach. Another popular way to   228
make the excursion of the continent is by train. These are modern and   242
quite efficient. They are dependable and reliable and in Europe are   256
a competitive form of transportation.   264

Most of all you will enjoy the people. When you meet them and   278
talk with them, you will be able to exchange ideas, make new friends,   292
and share opinions whether they be political or social. You will come   306
away with new concepts that will allow you to appreciate your home-   320
land in a way you would have never imagined.   329

| 1 | 2 | 3 | 4 | 5 | 6 | 7 | 8 | 9 | 10 | 11 | 12 | 13 | 14 | TOTAL WORDS

LESSON 4

LEFT-SHIFT FOR RIGHT-SIDE CAPITALS

NEW KEYS C V B AND LEFT SHIFT KEY

OBJECTIVE: To review the letters previously learned and to learn 3 new keys and the use of the left shift key.

DIRECTIONS: Place fingers on the home row keys of asdf jkl;. Type each of the following lines 3 times, double-spacing between each set of 3 lines.

MARGINS: 40-space line
SINGLE SPACING

REMEMBER to shift when you capitalize, using the little finger. Use the left shift key to capitalize any letter on the right side of the keyboard and vice versa. If you want to type in all caps, lock the shift key.

4-1 REVIEW

```
a;a sls dkd fjf dkd sls a;a sls dkd fjf
ded kik fgf jhj eee ddd iii kkk ffg jjh
deed furs kids lids fish fuss hide gird
```

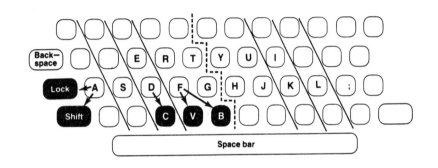

4-2 NEW REACHES

C Key: ddd dcd ccc ddd dcd ccc ddd ded ccc ded
V Key: fff fvf vvv fff fvf vvv fff fvf vvv fvf
B Key: fff fbf bbb fff fbf bbb fff fbf bbb fbf
Left Shift
Key: Lisa Lisa Kurt Kurt Jude Jude Hall Hall

4-3 USING THE NEW KEYS

```
dcd cdc car car child child dcd dcd cdc
dec ced frv vfr fbf bfb bbb ccc ddd fbf
fff vvv five five race race hives hives
fff bbb bills bills belt belt bask bask
```

4-4 ADDED PRACTICE

```
Jill said Lila hurt Kurt; Jeff Kyle Lee
Jeff called his father; Jesse Kerr fell
Karl led Judy here; say it is true blue
Jeff had five fish; Les had just three;
```

TIMING 1

	TOTAL WORDS
Of all the subjects that one studies in secondary school,	14
there are several that would benefit everyone whether or not they	28
are planning to attend college. The first one is typewriting.	42
This skill is now often called "keyboarding" and is considered a	56
necessity for operating a computer or word processor besides the	70
older skill advantages derived from knowing how to type.	82
For those going on to college, there will be many times when	96
you will need to type reports, themes, or term papers. If you	110
had to pay someone to do this for you each time it had to be	124
done, it would add significantly to your expenses. It would also	138
make you dependent on someone else to do the work at their con-	152
venience. Besides, learning the skill very well would enhance	166
your ability to compose, which in turn would save much time and	180
energy.	182
Another course that would be practical would be one that in-	196
cluded information on how to take notes and how to study. Such a	210
course would allow you to develop several important skills. You	224
would learn how to pick out the important facts when you read,	238
how to read faster, and how to underline correctly the informa-	252
tion in a book you need to remember. You would also learn to	266
take notes in outline form and how to pick out what is important	280
enough to write down.	285
Finally you learn how to study for examinations. There are	299
several hints and methods that would be beneficial because they	313
could save you hours of unnecessary reading or memorizing.	326
If any of these courses are offered in your school, you	339
should definitely consider taking them. You will probably find	353
them to be the most practical courses you will have studied.	366

TIMING 2

	TOTAL WORDS
After the long winter, one annually wonders at the marvel of how	14
nature knows that it is time to begin the life cycle all over again.	28
Spring is a glorious time of year. It is an amazing, exciting, and	42
invigorating experience.	47
In the rural areas--in the country and the towns--all sorts of	61
magical things begin to take place. There is fishing; there is swim-	75
ming; there is hiking; there is flower gathering; there is the town	89
picnic; there is dancing; and there is singing. Everywhere, people	103
welcome spring.	106
In the cities, which generally don't have all the signs of nature	120
that indicate the beginning of the season, there are special signs.	134
On the first warm day, the people open their apartment windows, sit on	148
the stoops, take evening walks in the city streets, visit the park,	162
take a ride on the carousel, buy a balloon and sip a cold soda being	176
sold by a street vendor. For people in the city, spring is also a	190
sort of magic--a magic that comes almost instantly as if to say that	204
the quality of city living has improved.	212
The days become longer in spring. Just one or two extra hours of	226
sunlight mean so much to people after a hard day on the job because	240
they like so much to sit out in their backyards or in their gardens or	254
on their terraces. It is so much nicer to relax outdoors rather than	268
indoors after the season has really begun.	276
The most important part in the human experience of the welcoming	290
of spring is the belief that one has a second chance, a new beginning,	304
and a reason for being. It is an appreciation of life and an appreci-	318
ation of our existence. It is the time of renewal; it is the time for	332
love. It is spring.	336

LESSON 5

OBJECTIVE: To review and reinforce the keys you have previously learned.

REVIEW

GOAL: To type 10 or more wpm* with no more than 1 error per minute.

KEEP AN EVEN TOUCH.

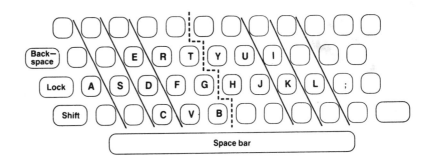

DIRECTIONS: Place fingers on the home row keys of asdf jkl;. Type each of the following lines 3 times, double-spacing between each set of 3 lines.

MARGINS: 40-space line
SINGLE SPACING

5-1

```
jjj fff kkk ddd lll sss ;;; aaa ggg hhh
juj frf ded kik jyj ftf dcd fbf ask lad
see Les tug sag hag the his gal hug Jeb
rug did dry ark tar ear tea eat yes rat
```

5-2

```
has gas kid Jed gay jet rid fur fed hid
less sulk dill fury Hale gash Kurt list
bury very Lill bash subs this just dirt
lest Lara bury tray skid dish salt sure
```

To measure your progress, you will now begin to take timed writings. First, reread the explanation on timing in the Introduction to this book. Then type each line as directed, repeating the copy until the minute ends. Use an automatic timer or a watch with a second-hand. Then enter your best score (most number of words per minute with fewest errors) in your Progress Chart.

DIRECTIONS: Practice each line 2 times; then take a 1-minute timed writing on it, repeating copy as necessary, with 10 wpm and no more than 1 error as your goal.

MARGINS: 50-space line
SINGLE SPACING

5-3 TIMED PRACTICE

```
Lisa hugs Jess; Jay heats the tea; take this test;   10
Jeff sulks; ask Harry; a sad lass talks; great day   10
these dukes ruled us fairly; Jill sits beside Katy   10
It is true reds are dark hues; grays are less dark   10

|  1  |  2  |  3  |  4  |  5  |  6  |  7  |  8  |  9  |  10  |
```

---
*words per minute

Timing 6

technology	profound	globe	Asia — even
communication	continent	orbit	satellites
interdependence	Tokyo	brighter	intertwined
political	nationalistic	Man's	twelve
economic	orientations	understanding	zones

Timing 7

mindset	beginning	artist	perfectly
nurtured	stumbling	endeavor	task
don't	blocks	Regardless	practice
accomplish	perform	shouldn't	ourselves
limitations	attempt	mercy	succeed

Timing 8

decades	young	automobile	phenomenon
suburbs	discovered	architecture	superhighways
"outtowns"	generation	theaters	viable
shopping	development	museums	vitality
redevelopment	efficient	interesting	behold

Timing 9

Babriel	America	Metric	planned
France	convert	medical	rigid
Australia	conversion	manufacturing	officially
Canada	adults	additional	basically
England	lazy	effort	1990's

Timing 10

happened	decrease	knowledgeable	improvement
business?	extreme	merchandise	accurately
vehicle	nowadays	satisfied	Perhaps
crowded	search	"thank you"	supermarket
self-servers	questions	rapid	clerk

LESSON 6

OBJECTIVE: To review the letters previously learned and to learn 4 new keys.

DIRECTIONS: Place fingers on the home row keys. Type each of the following lines 3 times, double-spacing between each set of 3 lines.

MARGINS: 40-space line
SINGLE SPACING

REMEMBER to space once after a comma.

DIRECTIONS: Practice each line 2 times; then take a 1-minute timed writing on it, repeating copy as necessary, with 10 wpm and no more than 1 error as your goal.

MARGINS: 50-space line
SINGLE SPACING

NEW KEYS
N M , :

GOAL: To type 10 or more wpm with no more than 1 error per minute.

6-1 REVIEW

```
jail dale rail haul list jest kale deal
keel seek jury duty sale sail real tile
flit risk rill jell raid gild such hail
```

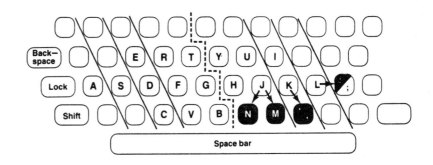

6-2 NEW REACHES

```
N Key: jjj jnj nnn jjj jnj nnn jjj jnj nnn jjj
M Key: jjj jmj mmm jjj jmj mmm jjj jmj mmm jmj
, Key: kkk k,k ,,, kkk k,k ,,, kkk k,k ,,, k,k
: Key: Use : as the shift of the ; key;  ;:;:;
```

6-3 USING THE NEW KEYS

```
jnj njn nnn ban nab and and Jen Jen nil
jmj mjm mmm mad dam man met Meg Meg ham
k,k ,k, ,,, ju, ft, ki, dc, jh, fg, k,k
at, it: ti, me, in: an, my, be: if, is,
```

6-4 TIMED PRACTICE

```
as, it, an, am, in, if, be, by, me, may, hem, aim:   10
me, end be, Ken my, fan in, ham as, men, den, ban,   10
Kim ran at ten; Huck came in last; Nancy had left;   10
Hal hid the bugs in the jug; Len is here at eight;    10
```

```
| 1 | 2 | 3 | 4 | 5 | 6 | 7 | 8 | 9 | 10 |
```

EXTENDED TIMED WRITINGS

After learning the keyboard, you should begin the practice once a week of taking extended timed writings for periods of 3 or 5 minutes. The 5 timings that appear in this section can be repeated as many times as necessary, in part or in whole.

If you have a timing mechanism handy, just set it for the time you wish to type; and when the bell rings, stop typing. If you only have a clock or watch available, you will have to look up every now and then to see how much time has elapsed.

GOALS

In any timing, your goal should be to have no more errors than the number of minutes you type. Thus, if you type for 3 minutes, there should be no more than 3 errors. If you type for 5 minutes, there should be no more than 5 errors.

Always type for the period of time that you have set, regardless of the number of errors. Only in this way will you see where you have to concentrate your practice.

Note your progress by recording your accuracy and speed in these timings in the Extended Timed Writing Chart that follows.

PROCEDURE

1. Before taking a timing, read the material that is to be typed and then practice the PREVIEW WORDS for that timing. You will find these words in the pages that follow. Practice each word of the preview 5 times. Circle errors and practice again those words that were difficult for you.

> *NOTE:* You might find a practice trial run of the entire timing helpful. Remember to touch-type when being timed—and RELAX!

2. Set the left margin for a 70-space line. Clear the right margin because you will follow the material line for line.
3. Put the line-space regulator on DOUBLE spacing.
4. Set a 5-space TAB indention.
5. Follow the material line for line. If you are able to complete the entire timing before the time limit, begin the timing again.
6. Take each timing 3 times. After each time, proofread carefully and circle your errors. Practice your errors after each timing by practicing the word before the error, the error itself (corrected), and the word after the error 3 times BEFORE taking the timing again.
7. Choose the best timing. The one that has the most words typed within the error limit should be chosen as the best of a series.

COMPUTING THE SCORE OF TIMINGS

For each timing or for the best timing of a series:

1. Find the last COMPLETE LINE in the TEXT that you typed. Note the number on the scale on the RIGHT. Write that number down.
2. Find the last INCOMPLETE LINE in the TEXT that you typed. Put your finger at where you stopped. Run your finger to the scale at the top or bottom. *Add* this number to the first.
3. *Divide* the total word count of the complete and incomplete lines by the number of minutes you typed. Give yourself an extra word for any fraction more than half.

PREVIEW WORDS

These should be practiced 5 times in succession across a line BEFORE taking a timing for the first time. Note how some of the words from the preview to Timing 1 would appear on the page:

subjects subjects subjects subjects subjects

probably probably probably probably probably

beneficial beneficial beneficial beneficial beneficial

typewriting typewriting typewriting typewriting typewriting

Timing 1

typewriting	significantly	important	probably
"keyboarding"	convenience	correctly	definitely
necessity	enhance	examinations	expenses
processor	practical	unnecessary	pick
themes	underline	memorizing	studied

Timing 2

winter	Everywhere	magic—	relax
marvel	apartment	instantly	human
cycle	carousel	spring	experience
amazing	balloon	backyards	appreciation
invigorating	soda	terraces	existence

Timing 3

forty	feasibility	"trolleys"	switch
streetcars	electricity	varieties	right-of-way
congested	energy-conscious	interurban	lightweight
bus	thirty	flattened	significant
underground	mechanical	overhead	transportation

Timing 4

broaden	Europe	museums	destinations
horizons	countries	enthralled	competitive
exciting	extraordinary	marvelous	transportation
differences	mountains	fascinated	opinions
life-styles	lifetin	quaint	imagined

Timing 5

companies	absenteeism	hobbies	disadvantages
America	four-day	younger	popular
experimenting	leisure	original	technology
workweek	personal	efficient	quality
employees	realize	don't	existence

LESSON 7

OBJECTIVE: To review the letters previously learned and to learn 4 new keys.

DIRECTIONS: Place fingers on the home row keys. Type each of the following lines 3 times, double-spacing between each set of 3 lines.

MARGINS: 40-space line
SINGLE SPACING

NEW KEYS
W X O .

GOAL: To type 11 or more wpm with no more than 1 error per minute.

REACH AND RETURN. THAT'S HOW TO LEARN!

7-1 REVIEW

```
jjn jjm kk, jnj jnj jmj jmj k,k i,k jnk
van van jam jam cake cake ask, ask, mad
and and mad mad sand sand made made nil
```

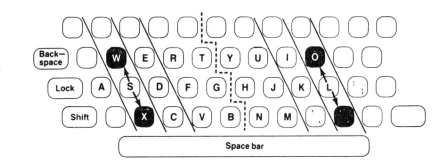

7-2 NEW REACHES

```
W Key: sss sws www sss sws www sss sws www sws
X Key: sss sxs xxx sss sxs xxx sss sxs xxx sxs
O Key: lll ·lol ooo lll lol ooo lll lol ooo lol
  Key: lll l.l ... lll l.l ... lll l.l ... l.l
```

7-3 USING THE NEW KEYS

```
sws wsw wish wish sun sun sing sing sws
sxs xsx mix mix exit exit six; six; fix
lol olo rod rod load load son son go go
l.l .l. ... fl. de. sx. as. ju. ki. l.l
```

Space twice after a period at the end of a sentence and once after a period used with an initial or after an abbreviation.

```
Mr. John O. Yuler was ill.
Maj. Barry is feeling fine.
```

DIRECTIONS: Practice each pair of lines 2 times; then take a 1-minute timed writing, repeating copy as necessary, with 11 wpm and no more than 1 error as your goal.

MARGINS: 30-space line
SINGLE SPACING

7-4 TIMED PRACTICE

```
wish wand lynx make silk crux    6
none mast vest text oxen keys   12

Lou ran.  He stayed.  I sang.    6
N. M. Long was out.  I am in.   12
```

```
|  1  |  2  |  3  |  4  |  5  |  6  |
```

WPM		DATE COMPLETED
95	You should never look when you type numbers using the upper row of keys. If you have practiced the reaches often enough and successfully enough, then you shouldn't have any problem. It is also important to proofread numbers very carefully for they must be exact in reports. Though words may be changed, numbers cannot. They have to be typed exactly and proofread exactly. One of the major errors made with numbers is their transposition which may occur.	10 20 30 40 50 60 70 80 90 95
100	If your goal has reached a point where you are practicing this paragraph, then you are an advanced student and a very good typist. Remember that all the zesty, quick speed in the world will not be satisfactory unless you are accurate too. Much time can be wasted in correcting any errors both large and small if you are too hasty and too careless in what you do. The quality of your work is essential to whether or not you are employable and to whether or not you will get promoted soon.	10 20 30 40 50 60 70 80 90 100

| | 1 | 2 | 3 | 4 | 5 | 6 | 7 | 8 | 9 | 10 | |

LESSON

8

OBJECTIVE: To review the letters previously learned and to learn 4 new keys and the use of the right shift key.

DIRECTIONS: Place fingers on the home row keys. Type each of the following lines 3 times, double-spacing between each set of 3 lines.

MARGINS: 40-space line
SINGLE SPACING

REMEMBER to use the right shift key whenever you capitalize a letter on the left side of the keyboard.

DIRECTIONS: Practice each pair of lines 2 times; then take a 1-minute timed writing, repeating copy as necessary, with 11 wpm and no more than 1 error as your goal.

MARGINS: 30-space line
SINGLE SPACING

NEW KEYS Q Z ' " AND RIGHT SHIFT KEY

GOAL: To type 11 or more wpm with no more than 1 error per minute.

8-1 REVIEW

```
saw saw lax lax dim dim six six box; ox;
mix mix jinx jinx exit exit next next ox
Neal is well.  Lynn came home.  I drive.
```

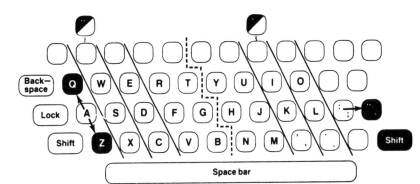

8-2 NEW REACHES

Q Key: aaa aqa qqq aaa aqa qqq aaa aqa qqq aqa
Z Key: aaa aza zzz aaa aza zzz aaa aza zzz aza

' Key
(electrics): ;'; ;'; ''' ;;; ''' ;;; ;'; ;'; ';' ';'

' Key
(manuals): The ' is the shift of the 8 key. 8'8'8

" Key
(electrics): The " is the shift of the ' key. '"'"'"

" Key
(manuals): The " is the shift of the 2 key. 2"2"2

Right Shift Key: Sam Flo Bob Sue Dad Zena Vera Gail Carl

8-3 USING THE NEW KEYS

```
aqaq quit quit quay quay aqua aqua aqaq
azaz zero zero quiz quiz zinc zinc azaz
aaa aqa aaa aza qaz Zeb '"'" zaq aza qaq
Walt Walt Zena Zena Edie Seth Edie Vera
```

8-4 TIMED PRACTICE

```
Sue quit her job.  Zeke ran in.      6
Zoe swam to shore.  A box fell.     12

Dolly fixed the box.  Quiz her.      6
Twelve quiet oxen ate the meat.     12
```

```
 |  1  |  2  |  3  |  4  |  5  |  6  |
```

WPM		DATE COMPLETED
75	Even after you know how to type well, it will sometimes be important for you to sit down at a new machine. The touch of the keyboard may feel different when you start. It is then a good idea to practice. Use one-minute timings; use five-minute timings. Move slowly at first until your fingers get used to making new reaches. Then pick up slowly the speed used.	10 20 30 40 50 60 70 75
80	You should always feel proud by the skill you have developed. To be able to typewrite and keyboard efficiently is one skill that will have many uses. It will serve you personally and professionally. It can keep you in steady employment. If you take the time to look at newspapers, you will clearly see that there are jobs out there for anyone qualified and looking for new opportunities.	10 20 30 40 50 60 70 80
85	If you apply for a position that requires the use of this skill, you will probably be asked to take a timed writing. The company will give you a few minutes to practice so that you can get used to the typewriter. Try to remember your good typing techniques. Try to put accuracy ahead of high speed, but don't flounder or get nervous if you make a few errors. If you do this, then you will probably make more errors.	10 20 30 40 50 60 70 80 85
90	Have you learned to type your numbers as well as your letters? Much of today's work involves typing numbers, and the ability to do this should be second nature for the good worker. Some computers have special numeric pads that make it easier to include numbers in lists or in reports. Self-confidence is the key to typing numbers and even symbols for that matter. Numbers are used more than names in product identification or in codes.	10 20 30 40 50 60 70 80 90

| 1 | 2 | 3 | 4 | 5 | 6 | 7 | 8 | 9 | 10 |

LESSON 9

OBJECTIVE: To review the letters previously learned and to learn 3 new keys.

DIRECTIONS: Place fingers on the home row keys. Type each of the following lines 3 times, double-spacing between each set of 3 lines.

MARGINS: 40-space line
SINGLE SPACING

THE DIAGONAL KEY is used with no space before or after.

REMEMBER to space twice after the ? at the end of a question.

DIRECTIONS: Practice each pair of lines 2 times; then take a 1-minute timed writing, repeating copy as necessary, with 12 wpm and no more than 1 error as your goal.

MARGINS: 30-space line
SINGLE SPACING

NEW KEYS P / ?

GOAL: To type 12 or more wpm with no more than 1 error per minute.

9-1 REVIEW

```
quiz quiz maze maze Carl Carl oxen zero
worn worm loam swam laze quit quit hazy
oxen haze Zena aqua exit daze gaze zinc
```

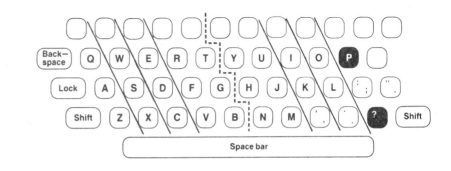

9-2 NEW REACHES

```
P Key:  ;;; ;p; ppp ;;; ;p; ppp ;;; ;p; ppp ;p;
/ Key:  ;;; ;/; /// ;;; ;/; /// ;;; ;/; /// ;/;
? Key:  The ? key is the shift of the /.  ;?;?;?
```

9-3 USING THE NEW KEYS

```
;;; ppp ;;; ppp ;/; ;/; /// /// ;/; ;p;
pal; pen; pro/con ape; she/her pal; pen
pony Paul more/less his/hers pace; pull
Can Paul run?  Will I walk?  Is Ben in?
```

9-4 TIMED PRACTICE

```
Paul pulled in this pure pelt.    6
Pete called; Pat had the pole.   12

Please put paper in here, Pam.    6
Poll pupils.  Call the police.   12


|  1  |  2  |  3  |  4  |  5  |  6  |
```

WPM		DATE COMPLETED
50	Try to practice every day when you are learning a new skill. In some drills you will need to try to be accurate while in other drills you will need to push for speed. Whichever your goal, it is best to try to make a little progress each day.	10 20 30 40 50
55	Using the keyboard on a computer is a fact of life today. Although it is larger and has more keys, the basic reaches remain the same. There are still the homerow keys from which you make all other reaches. It will save you much time if you operate a computer by touch.	10 20 30 40 50 55
60	When you try to improve your speed, do not worry about accuracy. Do not care if you make errors. Push as hard as you can to gain that extra stroke. Do not be happy until you have met your goal. If your fingers get out of control, slow down or pause for a second and then move on.	10 20 30 40 50 60
65	Try to set some time aside every day for practicing. It is just like playing a musical instrument. It is better to practice every day for short periods of time rather than every other day for longer periods. The ability to discipline oneself brings success. Daily reinforcement is the best way to improve.	10 20 30 40 50 60 65
70	You will see that your typing skill will improve without you realizing it. Your control will improve to the point where you will find yourself typing whole words without even thinking. The keys will simply seem to move all by themselves. You will be accurate, and you will be quick at the same time. Your skill will become well defined.	10 20 30 40 50 60 70

| 1 | 2 | 3 | 4 | 5 | 6 | 7 | 8 | 9 | 10 |

LESSON 10

USE QUICK, SHARP STROKES.

REVIEW

GOAL: To type 12 or more wpm with no more than 1 error per minute.

OBJECTIVE: To review and reinforce the keys you have previously learned.

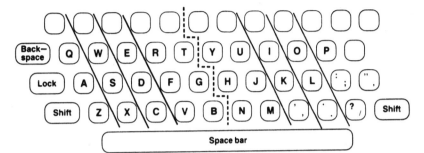

DIRECTIONS: Place fingers on the home row keys. Type each of the following lines 3 times, double-spacing between each set of 3 lines.

MARGINS: 40-space line
SINGLE SPACING

10-1

```
nail male sane maze nose lime dune June
wine oxen sexy whom hose exit next jinx
quit zero Dave some swab line lynx quip
pill pace type coax clad skid just Gina
each from swim cash step fuse gird Cora
```

10-2

```
dear hear word have like call help care
sir can fun the tub you lot you not won
thin will hold ball Dick Mary frog hold
water heavy person spike first learn be
```

DIRECTIONS: Practice each pair of lines 2 times; then take a 1-minute timed writing, repeating copy as necessary, with 12 wpm and no more than 1 error as your goal.

MARGINS: 30-space line
SINGLE SPACING

10-3 TIMED PRACTICE

```
We spoke.  Mark called up Meg.    6
Lois will come.  Ken told her.   12

Nell can sew.  Eve might help.    6
Joe plays golf; my dad paints.   12
```

```
|  1  |  2  |  3  |  4  |  5  |  6  |
```

WPM		DATE COMPLETED
15	It is really fun to learn to type on a type-writer. It is so easy.	10 15
20	One of the reasons you are learning to type is so that you will be able to type and not look.	10 20
25	Good posture is important to good typing. Your feet should be flat on the floor at all times and your eyes on the copy.	10 20 25
30	When pushing for typing speed, it is impor-tant to type faster and faster and faster. Do not worry about errors. Just keep on moving the keys.	10 20 30
35	It is important to be an accurate typist as well as it is to be a fast typist. The two goals go hand in hand. It is not good to be typing so fast that you make errors.	10 20 30 35
40	The best way to type without making errors is to let your eyes glide across the page letter by letter. Do not read the copy too quickly because you may forget to type one or two letters of copy.	10 20 30 40
45	Have you reached your goal in each of the lessons that you have typed? Has your speed been faster by one, two, or three words? Have you been able to maintain your accuracy by not making too many typewriting errors?	10 20 30 40 45

| 1 | 2 | 3 | 4 | 5 | 6 | 7 | 8 | 9 | 10 |

LESSON 11

OBJECTIVE: To review the letters previously learned and to learn 4 number and 4 symbol keys.

DIRECTIONS: Place fingers on the home row keys. Type each of the following lines 3 times, double-spacing between each set of 3 lines.

MARGINS: 40-space line
SINGLE SPACING

REMEMBER: You should learn the number keys as well as you now know the letter keys. Typing numbers rapidly and accurately is very important, especially if you should have occasion to use the latest electronic and word-processing equipment.

NUMBER KEYS 4 5 6 7; SYMBOL KEYS $ % ¢ &

GOAL: To type 13 or more wpm with no more than 1 error per minute.

11-1 REVIEW

```
ask lad saw lid dig him gun ear oil urn
yet toy quiz pose zeal mild fair sod so
vice boys bird exit cave gold sane bail
```

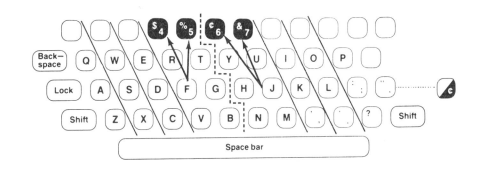

11-2 NEW REACHES

```
4 Key:  fff f4f 444 fff f4f 444 fff f4f 444 f4f
5 Key:  fff f5f 555 fff f5f 555 fff f5f 555 f5f
6 Key:  jjj j6j 666 jjj j6j 666 jjj j6j 666 j6j
7 Key:  jjj j7j 777 jjj j7j 777 jjj j7j 777 j7j
```

11-3 USING THE NEW KEYS

```
fr4f ju7j fr5f ju6j fr44 ju66 fr55 ju77
4455 6677 4454 6676 5545 7767 4567 7654
4 and 5 and 6 and 7; 45 and 46 and 477;
May 5; June 4; July 7; I am 5; I am 67;
```

11-4 SYMBOL KEYS

$ Key:	The $ is the shift of the 4 key. f$ff;
% Key:	The % sign is used often. f%f f%f 5%5;
¢ Key (electrics):	The ¢ key is the shift of the 6. j¢j¢j
¢ Key (manuals):	The ¢ key is next to the semicolon. ;¢
& Key:	The & sign is called the ampersand. j&

SKILL DEVELOPMENT ONE-MINUTE TIMINGS

GOAL   Type each paragraph within one minute without any errors. When you reach this goal, sign and date the column on the right and then move on to the next paragraph.

> *NOTE:* You must type for the full minute. If you complete the paragraph before that time, start over. Return twice and indent as if it were a new paragraph. This segment, too, must have total accuracy for your goal to be reached.

PROCEDURE   Use a 60-space line and single spacing. Set a five-space tab indention.

SKILL DEVELOPMENT

3 FOR ACCURACY

1. Type your paragraph three times for ACCURACY. Aim for the perfect timing, but try not to make more than one error. If you complete it before one minute, start over. All of the typing must have perfect copy in order to have the paragraph signed.

3 FOR SPEED

2. Type your paragraph three times for SPEED. Do not count errors. Go faster and faster each time. DO NOT USE THIS SPEED SEGMENT FOR REACHING YOUR GOAL.

3 FOR CONTROL

3. Type your paragraph three times for CONTROL. Slow down and try to make the goal.

4. Remember: a timing with one error does not count towards the goal. Stay on the same paragraph until you have no errors. If you reach this goal, initial and date the column to the right of the paragraph before moving on.

> *NOTE:* It is better to have someone time you. Use good typing techniques at all times.

DIRECTIONS: Practice each pair of lines 2 times; then take a 1-minute timed writing, repeating copy as necessary, with 13 wpm and no more than 1 error as your goal.

MARGINS: 35-space line
SINGLE SPACING

11-5 TIMED PRACTICE

```
The order came to $74.   We own 56%.    7
Write to Hoade, Walter, Jones & Co.    14

Try to buy 4 for 54¢, or 6 for 64¢.    7
Visit on May 14, June 5, or July 6.    14


 I  1  I  2  I  3  I  4  I  5  I  6  I  7  I
```

SKILL
DEVELOPMENT
AND
EXTENDED
TIMED
WRITINGS

LESSON 12

OBJECTIVE: To review the letters and numbers previously learned and to learn 4 new number and symbol keys.

DIRECTIONS: Place fingers on the home row keys. Type each of the following lines 3 times, double-spacing between each set of 3 lines.

MARGINS: 40-space line
SINGLE SPACING

NUMBER KEYS 3 8; SYMBOL KEYS # *

GOAL: To type 13 or more wpm with no more than 1 error per minute.

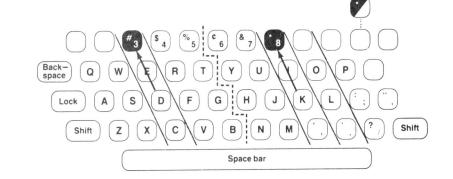

NUMBERS ARE IMPORTANT!

12-1 REVIEW

```
fff f4f jjj j6j fff f5f jjj j7j 444 777
456 645 764 476 567 457 654 657 546 574
fr4f ju6j fr5r ju7j fr44 ju77 fr55 jy66
```

12-2 NEW REACHES

3 Key: ddd d3d 333 ddd d3d 333 ddd d3d 333 d3d
8 Key: kkk k8k 888 kkk k8k 888 kkk k8k 888 k8k

12-3 USING THE NEW KEYS

```
d3d 3d3 333 ddd 345 737 436 473 436 537
k8k 8k8 888 kkk 834 748 853 884 384 538
38 and 83 and 38 and 38; 453; 883; 388;
45 and 46 and 47 and 48; 683; 846; 478;
```

12-4 SYMBOL KEYS

Key: The # is the shift of the 3 key.   d#d#;
* Key:
(electrics): The * is the shift of the 8 key.   k*k*;
* Key
(manuals): The * is the shift of the hyphen. —**—

DIRECTIONS: Practice each pair of lines 2 times; then take a 1-minute timed writing, repeating copy as necessary, with 13 wpm and no more than 1 error as your goal.

MARGINS: 35-space line
SINGLE SPACING

12-5 TIMED PRACTICE

```
Kate held No. 8388; David held 683.      7
The order came July 3; buy 38 ties.     14

Mark sold 338 books.  Alex sold 78.      7
Pick out 83 pens.  Keep 48 of them.     14
```

```
| 1 | 2 | 3 | 4 | 5 | 6 | 7 |
```

DIRECTIONS: Compose at the typewriter a data sheet for yourself that is similar to either of the samples in Problems 60-1 or 60-2. Proofread, edit, and revise it. Then retype the corrected copy with one carbon, to keep for future reference.

REMEMBER: Proofread and make all corrections carefully. Since your data sheet is a reflection of you, it must be accurate, well typed, and neat in appearance.

DIRECTIONS: Take a 1-minute timing on the control paragraph, repeating copy as necessary. Remember, your goal is to type it at 45 wpm with no more than 1 error per minute.

MARGINS: 70-space line
SINGLE SPACING

60-3

(Use the form on Worksheet 5 to set up the first draft of your personal data sheet before typing the final draft.)

SKILL IMPROVEMENT

(Refer to the Skill Improvement exercise in LESSON 40.)

LESSON 13

OBJECTIVE: To review the letters and numbers previously learned and to learn 4 new number and symbol keys.

DIRECTIONS: Place fingers on the home row keys. Type each of the following lines 3 times, double-spacing between each set of 3 lines.

MARGINS: 40-space line
SINGLE SPACING

NUMBER KEYS 2 9; SYMBOL KEYS @ (

CHECK YOUR POSTURE.

GOAL: To type 14 or more wpm with no more than 1 error per minute.

13-1 REVIEW

```
ddd d3d kkk k8k ddd d3d kkk k8k 333 888
435 384 583 683 865 383 477 655 838 333
4/7/78; 3/8/74; more/less; pro/con; ;/;
```

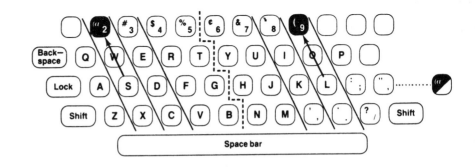

13-2 NEW REACHES

2 Key: sss s2s 222 sss s2s 222 sss s2s 222 s2s
9 Key: 111 191 999 111 191 999 111 191 999 191

13-3 USING THE NEW KEYS

```
s2s 2s2 222 sss s2s2 sw2s 2ws2 s2s 2s2s
191 919 999 111 1919 lo91 9ol9 191 9191
29 and 92 and 38; 83 and 45 and 67; 292
I am 29; he is 39; she is 75; he is 64.
```

13-4 SYMBOL KEYS

@ Key (electrics): The @ key is the shift of the 2. s@@s;
@ Key (manuals): The @ key is the shift of the ¢. ;@;p@
(Key: The (key is the shift of the 9. l((9;

DIRECTIONS: Practice each pair of lines 2 times; then take a 1-minute timed writing, repeating copy as necessary, with 14 wpm and no more than 1 error as your goal.

MARGINS: 35-space line
SINGLE SPACING

13-5 TIMED PRACTICE

```
Flight 293 may come about 9:45 a.m.      7
Ed can scrub Tables 29, 37, and 39.     14

Train 92 will leave about 8:35 p.m.      7
William will meet me at 5:25 today.     14
```

```
| 1 | 2 | 3 | 4 | 5 | 6 | 7 |
```

DIRECTIONS: Make a copy of this data sheet for Virginia Smith. Center it vertically on a full sheet of paper. Line-space according to the format in the sample. Proofread your copy carefully and correct all errors.

NOTE: There are several differences between the layout of this data sheet and that of the previous problem. Notice that the work experience is listed before the education and that there is more detailed explanation of duties performed.

MARGINS: 6-inch line
SINGLE SPACING

VIRGINIA SMITH
4902 Jerome Avenue
Wilmington, DE 19802

Tel: (302) 555-3025

OCCUPATIONAL OBJECTIVE:

    Administrative Advertising Assistant--Marketing Research Analyst

WORK EXPERIENCE:

    9/76 to present Keenan Advertising Agency, 504 Chestnut Street, Wilmington, DE 19824

                      Prepared market research projects in order to determine the need for advertising, including sales potential. Had experience in writing detailed reports, including step-by-step recommendations for sales development and sales improvements. Continued development of skill in drawing rough sketches of advertising layouts.

    7/75 to 8/76   Thomas Advertising Associates, 302 Market Street, Wilmington, DE 19804

                      Material Coordinator and Administrative Assistant. Handled all correspondence and kept advertising records and reports of clients. Prepared advertising reports of prospective clients. Had an opportunity to prepare sketches of proposed advertising layouts.

EDUCATION:

    Pierre Dupont High School, Wilmington, 1968-1971, academic diploma

    Delaware State College, Dover, 1971-1975, B.S. in Business Administration

            Major: Economics and Marketing
            Minor: Accounting and Secretarial Science

    Central Art Academy, Wilmington, 1977-1979, part-time student in advertising layout design

HOBBIES:

    Photography, drawing, writing, sports, and travel

REFERENCES:

    These will be furnished upon request.

LESSON 14

OBJECTIVE: To review the letters and numbers previously learned and to learn 2 new number and 5 new symbol keys.

DIRECTIONS: Place fingers on the home row keys. Type each of the following lines 3 times, double-spacing between each set of 3 lines.

MARGINS: 40-space line
SINGLE SPACING

USE the hyphen as a minus (−) symbol.

USE the hyphen and colon to make the division (÷) symbol.
    Type hyphen -
    Backspace
    Type colon ÷

TYPE the hyphen twice to make a dash (--).

NUMBER KEYS 1 0; SYMBOL KEYS) - = ＿ + ÷ !

GOAL: To type 14 or more wpm with no more than 1 error per minute.

14-1 REVIEW

```
sss s2s lll l9l sss s2s lll l9l 222 999
293 943 852 695 736 359 647 762 283 682
s2s l9l d3d k8k f4f j7j f5f j6j 222 999
```

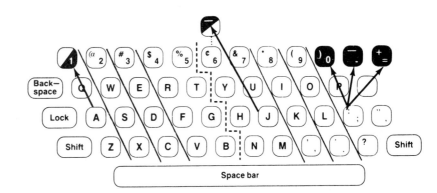

14-2 NEW REACHES

> NOTE: Most typewriters have a key for Number 1; if yours does not, use the small "L."

1 Key:	aaa ala lll aaa ala lll aaa ala lll ala
0 Key:	;;; ;0; 000 ;;; ;0; 000 ;;; ;0; 000 ;0;
) Key:	The) key is the shift of the 0. 0))0)
- Key (hyphen):	;;; ;-; --- ;;; ;-; --- ;;; ;-; --- ;-;
= Key (equal):	;;; ;=; === ;;; ;=; === ;;; ;=; === ;=;
÷ (division):	4 ÷ 2 = 2; 16 ÷ 8 = 2; 10 ÷ 2 = 5; 100 ÷ 50 = 2

14-3 USING THE NEW KEYS

```
ala lal lll aaa I read lll pages.  lll;
;0; 0;0 lll 000 I am 10 years old.   000
Use the up-to-date books--use them well.
```

DIRECTIONS: Make a copy of this data sheet for John J. Jones. Center it vertically on a full sheet of paper. Line-space according to the format in the sample. Proofread your work carefully and correct all errors.

MARGINS: 6-inch line
SINGLE SPACING

JOHN J. JONES   (215) 555-3004
157 Baker Avenue South
Philadelphia, PA 19140-1572

<u>EDUCATION</u>:

1977-1983   Watson Elementary School
                 Philadelphia, PA

1983-1986   Jay Cooke Junior High School
                 Philadelphia, PA

1986-present   Central High School   (To graduate in
                 Philadelphia, PA   June, 1989)

<u>SPECIAL ACTIVITIES</u>:

    Member of the school debating team; participated in
    citywide contests

    Member of the intramural basketball team during my
    freshman and sophomore years in high school

    Assistant editor of the school newspaper, <u>The Clarion</u>

<u>WORK EXPERIENCE</u>:

Summer, 1986   Waiter-busboy in the Mountain Resort
                  Hotel in Mayville, Pennsylvania

9/86 to 9/87   Grocery Clerk, Cashier, and Checker, in
                  Spot Food Market, Cheltenham, Pennsylva-
                  nia

December, 1983   Sales Clerk for local variety store for
                  the Christmas season

<u>HOBBIES</u>:

    Swimming, boating, reading, sports, and science-fiction
    movies

<u>REFERENCES</u>:

    Mr. Arthur Hill, Manager, Mountain Resort Hotel, May-
    ville, Pennsylvania

    Miss Helen Keene, English teacher, Central High School,
    Philadelphia, Pennsylvania

    Mr. William Kramer, Coach, Central High School basket-
    ball team

14-4 MORE SYMBOL KEYS

__ Key
(electrics):   The underscore is the shift of the hyphen.

__ Key
(manuals):   The underscore is the shift of the 6.   6_6

+ Key
(plus):   The + sign is the shift of the = key.   +=+

! (exclamation
point)   Run! Skip! Jump! Play! Cheer! Don't Walk!

REMEMBER to underscore solidly un-less you want to add emphasis to each word. Type words to be under-scored, backspace to the point the underscore is to begin, press the shift key, and underscore. Do not under-shoot or overshoot the word or words.

USE the apostrophe and period to make the exclamation point (!).
  Type apostrophe '
  Backspace
  Type period !
  Leave 2 spaces after an exclamation point.

14-5 ADDITIONAL NUMBER AND SYMBOL PRACTICE

DIRECTIONS: Place fingers on the home row keys. Type each of the following lines 3 times, double-spacing between each set of 3 lines.

USE + for addition.

Add 3 + 4 + 2 + 9 = 18; Add 2 + 7 + 5 + 6 = 20.

USE — (hyphen) for subtraction.

Subtract: 1,000 — 500 = 500; 1,250 — 1,250 = 0.

USE small x for multiplication.

Multiply: 2 x 13; 4 x 18; 5 x 5; 7 x 8; 4 x 65.

USE hyphen backspace colon for division.

Divide: 44 ÷ 2 = 22; 88 ÷ 44 = 2; 100 ÷ 2 = 50.

Leave 1 space after ;
  2 spaces after :
  1 space before and after + — × ÷

Don't walk too fast! Run quickly! Listen now!

14-6 TIMED PRACTICE

DIRECTIONS: Practice each pair of lines 2 times; then take a 1-minute timed writing, repeating copy as necessary, with 14 wpm and no more than 1 error as your goal.

MARGINS: 35-space line
SINGLE SPACING

```
Are there 12 golf balls or just 10?   7
Please wait 15 days; he'll be here.   14

Mike sold 250--Billy sold only 193.   7
There (in the box) are 101 pencils.   14

 I  1  I  2  I  3  I  4  I  5  I  6  I  7  I
```

LESSON 60

OBJECTIVE: To learn how to prepare and type your own personal data sheet when applying for a job.

DIRECTIONS: Type the warm-up line 3 times with <u>speed</u> as your goal.

MARGINS: 70-space line

PREPARING AND TYPING A PERSONAL DATA SHEET

GOAL: To type 45 or more wpm with no more than 1 error per minute.

CONGRATULATIONS— YOU'VE MET YOUR GOAL!

WARM-UP

The living standard in the United States of
America is still high now.

A personal data sheet (or resume) is prepared when one is looking for a job. It lists personal information, educational background, previous employment experience, and references. Personal data sheets can be prepared in many different ways. Therefore, it is wise to check reference sources for the style best suited to your needs.

The data sheet should be centered vertically on a full sheet of paper. You should try to have a 1-inch top and bottom margin. For a basic resume style, use a 6-inch writing line (60 spaces/pica, 72/elite), and line-space according to the sample in Problem 60-1.

NOTE:

- Education is listed in order of schools attended—from past to present.
- Job experience is listed in reverse order—working backwards from present to past.
- For each reference that appears, permission should be granted.

(Lesson 60 continued on next page.)

OBJECTIVE: To review and reinforce the keys you have previously learned.

DIRECTIONS: Type the warm-up line 3 times with <u>speed</u> as your goal.

MARGINS: 40-space line

REVIEW

GOAL: To type 15 or more wpm with no more than 1 error per minute.

DON'T LOOK AT YOUR FINGERS.

WARM-UP

James is too ill to play the game today.

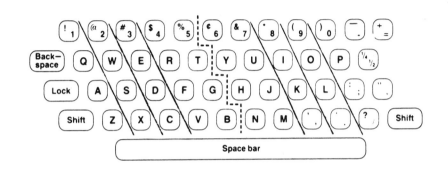

DIRECTIONS: Place fingers on the home row keys. Type each of the following lines 3 times, double-spacing between each set of 3 lines.

MARGINS: 40-space line
SINGLE SPACING

15-1

```
f4f  f4f  f4f  j7j  j7j  j7j  f5f  f5f  f5f  j6j
j6j  j6j  d3d  d3d  d3d  k8k  k8k  k8k  s2s  s2s
s2s  l9l  l9l  l9l  ala  ala  ala  ;0;  ;0;  ;0;
```

15-2

```
We sold 24 chairs, 3 tables, and 9 pots.
He baked 10 cakes, 12 pies, and muffins.
Mel saw 11 deer, 3 rabbits, and 4 foxes.
```

15-3

```
These gloves might cost at least $23.75.
Johnson & Johnson is a big-name company.
About 25% of the students will not come.
Train #38 and Flight #4 leave on Monday.
Eggs selling @ 75¢ a dozen are freshest.
```

DIRECTIONS: Practice each pair of lines 2 times; then take a 1-minute timed writing, repeating copy as necessary, with 15 wpm and no more than 1 error as your goal.

MARGINS: 40-space line
SINGLE SPACING

15-4 TIMED PRACTICE

```
The cold spell will last only five days.    8
Some people may enjoy the balmy weather.   16

Spring and fall are my favorite seasons.    8
Hurricane David did considerable damage.   16
```

```
|   1   |   2   |   3   |   4   |   5   |   6   |   7   |   8   |
```

Now that you have learned the keyboard, you should begin to take extended timed writings for periods of 3 to 5 minutes at least once a week. You will find directions and additional timed writings at the end of this book.

DIRECTIONS: Prepare a title page for a report or theme you might have occasion to write.

DIRECTIONS: Take a 1-minute timing on the control paragraph, repeating copy as necessary. Remember, your goal is to type it at 45 wpm with no more than 1 error per minute.

MARGINS: 70-space line
SINGLE SPACING

▶ SAMPLE 3 (PERSONAL BUSINESS REPORT)

1. Draw a warning line in pencil 1 inch from the bottom of the paper, and also lightly mark the vertical center of the page.
2. Beginning on line 13, center the title of the report. This may be in full caps.
3. Six lines below the vertical center you have marked, center and type "Prepared by." Double-space and center your name. Then double-space again and center your position and/or committee.
4. Turn the paper to the warning line and type the date. This may be centered or set off to the right of the page.

PERSONAL BUSINESS REPORT

59-1

(Follow the style of Samples 1, 2, or 3.)

SKILL IMPROVEMENT

(Refer to the Skill Improvement exercise in LESSON 39.)

CHAPTER

11

REFINING
KEYBOARD
SKILLS

LESSON 59

OBJECTIVE: To learn how to type a cover page for a manuscript.

DIRECTIONS: Type the warm-up line 3 times with <u>control</u> as your goal.

MARGINS: 70-space line

TYPING A TITLE PAGE

GOAL: To type 45 or more wpm with no more than 1 error per minute.

WARM-UP

In Philadelphia they signed the Declaration of
Independence willingly.

Procedure for Typing a Title Page

There are many different ways to type a title page for a report, theme, or other manuscript. Since many schools, colleges, and organizations use their own particular style, always check to see which style is preferred. Three samples are given here.

▶ *SAMPLE 1 (THEME)*

1. Draw a light pencil line 1 inch from the bottom of the paper.
2. On line 13, center the title of the report in full caps. You may spread-center the title if you wish.
3. Double-space; then center the word "by." Double-space again; then center and type your name.
4. Single-space 19 times and then center and type the name of the course. Double-space and center the time the class meets. Double-space and center the name of the instructor.
5. Return the paper to the warning line (see #1 above). Center and type the date on which the paper is due.

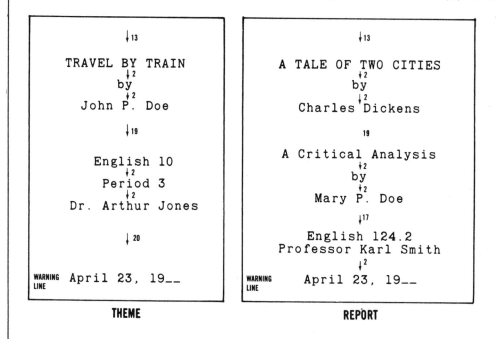

THEME   REPORT

▶ *SAMPLE 2 (REPORT)*

1. Draw a light pencil line 1 inch from the bottom of the paper.
2. On line 13, center the title of the book. This may be in full caps.
3. Double-space; then center the word "by." Double-space and center the name of the author.
4. Single-space 19 times and then center the type of assignment. Double-space and center "by." Double-space and center your name.
5. Turn the paper to the warning line, then go back 2 lines. Using single space, center and type the name of the course, the name of the instructor, and the date the paper is due.

LESSON 16

BALANCED HAND DRILLS

2 GOALS: ACCURACY AND SPEED

GOAL: To type 16 or more wpm with no more than 1 error per minute.

OBJECTIVE: To improve your typing proficiency using both hands.

DIRECTIONS: Type the warm-up line 3 times with <u>accuracy</u> as your goal.

MARGINS: 40-space line

DIRECTIONS: Place fingers on the home row keys. Type each of the following lines 3 times, double-spacing between each set of 3 lines.

MARGINS: 40-space line
SINGLE SPACING

DIRECTIONS: Practice each pair of lines 2 times; then take a 1-minute timed writing, repeating copy as necessary, with 16 wpm and no more than 1 error as your goal.

MARGINS: 40-space line
SINGLE SPACING

WARM-UP

He will try to come to see you at eight.

16-1

```
ale won did fry gin lea ask win hen can
amp ego use the its kin due ice ban but
who arm six two his not may way out had
```

16-2

```
mast wand same word oxen quit dine cane
late mice boat owed sent your form kite
exit omit comb wand have them most soap
```

16-3

```
court brown prize money dozen quota ace
equip ebony brain stock avoid comic due
quake above globe voice windy brain aid
```

16-4 TIMED PRACTICE

```
Flight No. 1158 lands tonight at 10 p.m.    8
Ask his firm to pay the fare for eleven.   16

Del Read has just quit my show and fled.    8
Gus made the team and will win tomorrow.   16
```

```
|  1  |  2  |  3  |  4  |  5  |  6  |  7  |  8  |
```

DIRECTIONS: Make a copy of this bibliography, using the procedure for a short bibliography and following your bell. Proofread carefully and correct all errors.

MARGINS: 6-inch line
SINGLE SPACING

58-1

BIBLIOGRAPHY

Baker, Joan L., and Martha Thompson. Travel for
    Mature Adults., New York:, Basic Book
    Company, Inc., 1983, pp. 67–82.

_____ . Charter Travel., Chicago: ˙ N. &
    R. Book Company, 1987, pp. 17–30.

Ryan, Robert N. "The New Resorts." Littleville
    Chronicle, February 2, 1985, pp. 1–3.

Swenson, David L. "Traveling Made Easy." Monthly
    Travel, Vol. IV, No. 2 (October, 1987),
    pp. 7–9

Williams, Peter. "Travel by Freighter." Inter-
    national Travel, Vol. III, No. 1 (May,
    1985), pp. 28–33.

DIRECTIONS: Entries should be arranged in alphabetical order by last name of author. If no author is known, use title of publication. Follow the same procedure as in 58-1.

58-2

Quaker, Alicia. "Special Considerations." ˑModern Views,
    Vol. II, No. 8 (September, 1987), pp. 4–9.

Numan, Simpson L. ˑUsing Public Transportation.. Dallas: Future
    Publishing, Inc., 1986, pp. 14– 20–35; 65.

Charles, Robert P. Life in the Big Cities. New York:. New Books,
    Inc., 1983, pp. 1–30.

Mathew, Irene and Joanne C. Seymour. "How to Rent an Apartment in
    a Big City." ˑCity Weekly. April 17, 1988, pp. 19–28.

Zuckerstein, Marian.ˑ "Utilizing Cities After Work." ˑYour City,
    Vol. VII, No. 10 (October, 1987), pp. 15–22.

_____ ˑ"Steering Your Way to Success." ˙Modern Views,
    Vol. I, No. 4 (April, 1986), pp. 37–43.

Utica, Johnson., Neighborhoods Can Be Enlightening.
    Los Angeles:. City Press Company, 1988, Chapter 3.˙

SKILL IMPROVEMENT

(Refer to the Skill Improvement exercise in LESSON 38.)

DIRECTIONS: Take a 1-minute timing on the control paragraph, repeating copy as necessary. Remember, your goal is to type it at 45 wpm with no more than 1 error per minute.

MARGINS: 70-space line
SINGLE SPACING

LESSON 17

RIGHT-HAND AND LEFT-HAND DRILLS

GOAL: To type 17 or more wpm with no more than 1 error per minute.

STROKE SMOOTHLY.

OBJECTIVE: To help you gain proficiency typing words using letters typed exclusively with the right hand, left hand, and alternate hands.

DIRECTIONS: Type the warm-up line 3 times with <u>control</u> as your goal.

MARGINS: 40-space line

DIRECTIONS: Place fingers on the home row keys. Type each of the following lines 3 times, double-spacing between each set of 3 lines.

MARGINS: 40-space line
SINGLE SPACING

DIRECTIONS: Practice each pair of lines 2 times; then take a 1-minute timed writing, repeating copy as necessary, with 17 wpm and no more than 1 error as your goal.

MARGINS: 45-space line
SINGLE SPACING

REMEMBER to space <u>twice</u> after the colon!

WARM-UP

One paper arrived in the mail late today.

17-1 LEFT HAND

eve saw was gas eat were teas reds vest
gate raft fact cart data stew bear crab
weave state grave dread reads brag west

17-2 RIGHT HAND

you oil hum nun ply noun kill yolk pump
hymn pony polo loin link mill upon jump
union hilly lumpy nymph onion noun hill

17-3 ALTERNATE HANDS

sew ion ate him ear you tar nil car inn
west pulp dare look fast mink rate milk
union serve jolly craze phony dear link

17-4 TIMED PRACTICE

Type these figures only: 85, 24, 11, and 13.   9
The usual prices for the chair were not paid.   18

Zeke read tales about their next big mission.   9
Jeffrey quickly gave his pals three quarters.   18

| 1 | 2 | 3 | 4 | 5 | 6 | 7 | 8 | 9 |

LESSON 58

OBJECTIVE: To learn how to prepare a bibliography.

DIRECTIONS: Type the warm-up line 3 times with <u>accuracy</u> as your goal.

MARGINS: 70-space line

PREPARING A BIBLIOGRAPHY

GOAL: To type 45 or more wpm with no more than 1 error per minute.

WARM-UP

```
Important people use all their resources hoping
they win much success.
```

Procedure for Typing a Bibliography

▶ *SHORT BIBLIOGRAPHY* (generally less than 10 entries)

1. Set margins for a 6-inch line (60 spaces/pica, 72/elite). Use single spacing. Set a 5- or 10-space tab indention.
2. Center and type the title BIBLIOGRAPHY in full caps on line 13. Return the carriage 3 times.
3. Begin the first line of an entry at the left margin. Indent each succeeding line 5 or 10 spaces.
4. Single-space within entries but double-space between.

▶ *LONG BIBLIOGRAPHY* (generally more than 10 entries)

1. Begin the title BIBLIOGRAPHY on line 13. Leave a 1-inch bottom margin. Use a 6-inch line.
2. If you need a second page, type the page number on line 7 at the right margin. Return 3 times and continue adding entries.
3. Follow all other steps for the short bibliography.

> *NOTE:* Remember that margins may vary with manuscripts, depending upon whether or not the manuscripts are to be bound. The 6-inch line is acceptable in most cases. If the manuscript is to be bound, move the left margin stop in 5 spaces. Be sure that margins set for both the bibliography and the footnotes (if set as "notes" on separate pages) correspond to the margins used in the body of the manuscript.

▶ *BIBLIOGRAPHY COMPOSITION*
(Refer to the sample bibliography in Problem 58-1.)

1. Major divisions are set off by periods.
2. Entries are listed alphabetically. An author's name is written in reverse order (last name first) unless there are two. In that case, the name of the second author may be written in natural order.
3. If an author's name is used more than once in an alphabetical listing, a line can be used to indicate this.
4. Titles of books, periodicals, and newspapers are underscored. Names of articles in periodicals and newspapers are placed in quotation marks.

LESSON

18

ADJACENT-LETTER DRILLS

RETURN THE CARRIAGE WITHOUT LOOKING.

GOAL: To type 18 or more wpm with no more than 1 error per minute.

OBJECTIVE: To become proficient in typing words using adjacent letters of the typewriter keyboard.

DIRECTIONS: Type the warm-up line 3 times with speed as your goal.

MARGINS: 40-space line

DIRECTIONS: Place fingers on the home row keys. Type each of the following lines 3 times, double-spacing between each set of 3 lines.

MARGINS: 40-space line
SINGLE SPACING

WARM-UP

```
Bill said he will come to the mall soon.
```

18-1

```
sorts frail graft fever brave bugle tiger
young junks thyme rajah major month hinge
edict erode drift cadet vocal bruin khaki
mower wrist sedan taxes excel choir local
```

18-2

```
straps thrift finger verify behave badger
taught youths jungle hybrid powers jumble
sullen shunts edible ermine deface candid
novice infuse kidnap wealth swamps dusted
```

DIRECTIONS: Practice each pair of lines 2 times; then take a 1-minute timed writing, repeating copy as necessary, with 18 wpm and no more than 1 error as your goal.

MARGINS: 45-space line
SINGLE SPACING

18-3 TIMED PRACTICE

```
On March 18 we may feed 123 boys and 110 men.    9
It is necessary to use all the time you need.   18

Send Judge Rabb to quiz five or six boys now.    9
You must add a quart of oil when you need it.   18
```

```
|  1  |  2  |  3  |  4  |  5  |  6  |  7  |  8  |  9  |
```

DIRECTIONS: Take a 1-minute timing on the control paragraph, repeating copy as necessary. Remember, your goal is to type it at 45 wpm with no more than 1 error per minute.

MARGINS: 70-space line
SINGLE SPACING

SKILL IMPROVEMENT

(Refer to the Skill Improvement exercise in LESSON 37.)

DOUBLE-LETTER DRILLS

ELBOWS IN; BACK STRAIGHT

GOAL: To type 19 or more wpm with no more than 1 error per minute.

OBJECTIVE: To become proficient in typing words containing double letters.

DIRECTIONS: Type the warm-up line 3 times with <u>accuracy</u> as your goal.

MARGINS: 40-space line

DIRECTIONS: Place fingers on the home row keys. Type each of the following lines 3 times, double-spacing between each set of 3 lines.

MARGINS: 40-space line
SINGLE SPACING

DIRECTIONS: Practice each pair of lines 2 times; then take a 1-minute timed writing, repeating copy as necessary, with 19 wpm and no more than 1 error as your goal.

MARGINS: 50-space line
SINGLE SPACING

WARM-UP

Strike the keys as if they were very hot.

19-1

```
ribbon rubber robber accord occurs succor
peddle oddity fiddle sleeps sweets needle
staffs effort sodden dagger really yellow
```

19-2

```
sunny banner cannot booked gloomy voodoos
appear ripped errors terror lesson assets
lessee matter attain butter nozzle passed
```

19-3 TIMED PRACTICE

```
Millie Ellis had to call three stubborn men today.    10
A good committee might help to insure our success.    20

Will most of the wood on that hill be cut for use?    10
Today one's barber might be called a hair stylist.    20
```

```
 |  1  |  2  |  3  |  4  |  5  |  6  |  7  |  8  |  9  |  10  |
```

The peoples of this hemisphere stand
in a special relationship . . . which
sets them apart from the rest of the
world born of the determination to
insulate America from Western Europe
and its perpetual broils.[1]

Basically the inter-American system is a set
of principles on which the allied countries rely
as the basis of their relations with each other
since these countries share the same feelings, ~~and~~
~~have in many cases common objectives.~~[2] Perhaps the
organization serves as discipline for the member
nations in that it helps to regulate and support
their relations with one another.[2] ~~relations which~~
~~add to mutual benefit.~~[2]

The world's oldest organization, it was con-
ceived by Bolivar. Its development came about because of the feelings of the need for peace and
security in the Western Hemisphere. The first
treaty between the Latin American States was
signed at the Congress of Panama in 1826. The
first international conference was held in Wasing-
ton, D. C., and it set up an exchange of commercial information under the name of the Commercial
Bureau. In 1910 this name was changed to the Pan
American Union, and in 1948 the name was changed
again--this time to the Organization of American
States. Under this new setup, the Pan American
Union was to be its permanent secretariat.[3]

Columbus, Ohio: [1]James Slater, The OAS and United States Foreign Policy (Ohio State University Press, 1967),
p. 265.

[2]John C. Drier, The Organization of American
States and the Hemisphere Crisis (New York: Har-
per & Row, 1962), pp. 11 and 12.

[3]Ibid.

LESSON 20

PARAGRAPH TYPING

INDENT 5 SPACES FOR A PARAGRAPH

GOAL: To type 20 or more wpm with no more than 1 error per minute.

OBJECTIVE: To improve your ability in typing material other than drills.

DIRECTIONS: Type the warm-up line 3 times with <u>control</u> as your goal.

MARGINS: 40-space line

WARM-UP

He will bring his boy to the game later.

To type the paragraphs in this lesson, you will need to know how to set a tab stop for a 5-space indention. The tab stop is used for indenting paragraphs and other operations in which you want to move the carriage rapidly to an assigned point without striking the space bar repeatedly. The *tab set key* is used to set the stop; the *tab clear key* is used to eliminate a stop previously set.

To indent a paragraph 5 spaces:

* First set the left margin.
* Clear any tab stops already set by pressing the tab clear key or moving the carriage to the right margin and returning it while pressing the clear key.
* Move the carriage to the point where a tab stop is to be set and press the tab set key.
* Be sure to test the setting by returning the carriage to the left margin and pressing the tab key or bar. The carriage should move immediately to the point where the tab is set.

Learn to Proofread

You should always proofread your work. When you proofread, follow this procedure:

* Always proofread *before* removing the paper from the typewriter.
* Use the paper bail as a ruler. Turn the cylinder knob line by line so that the line being proofread is just above the bail.
* At first, read slowly and carefully, word by word. Later, as you become more proficient, you will learn to take in phrases at a glance.
* Use a pencil to point to the words as you are reading.
* Circle your errors.

DIRECTIONS: Use a 5-space tab indention. Type the paragraph once. Then proofread it and circle your errors, using the procedure just described. Type correctly 3 times each word in which you had made an error. Retype the paragraph once with accuracy as your goal.

MARGINS: 50-space line
DOUBLE SPACING

20-1

We all need to know how to write well, as most of us may have a great deal of it to do in much of our work. It could easily be learned if we make up our mind to do so right now.

20-2

Unless you try at least two new things it will no doubt be hard for you to progress in a job. Value all you will be able to learn and try to improve daily. You may be pleased.

DIRECTIONS: Take a 1-minute timed writing on this paragraph with 20 wpm and no more than 1 error per minute as your goal. First read the paragraph; then practice it once before taking the timed writing.

MARGINS: 50-space line
SINGLE SPACING

20-3 TIMED PRACTICE

Your time is precious. How it is used can de- 10
termine if you will be successful. You should use 20
time wisely in order to gain the best use from it. 30
Never waste time in idleness. 36

| 1 | 2 | 3 | 4 | 5 | 6 | 7 | 8 | 9 | 10 |

ELLIPSES

Ellipses are used to indicate the omission of one or more words in material that has been quoted. They are typed with periods and spaces inserted between them.

▶ *WITHIN A SENTENCE:* Use 3 periods with a space before and after each.

```
     "I have never met a stream . . . and fortunately
nobody knows it."
```

▶ *AT THE END OF A SENTENCE:* Use 4 periods. The first period begins right after the last word. Spaces are inserted before and after the others. Should a quotation mark follow the last period, it should be typed right after it without a space.

```
     "Some birds are poets and sing all summer. They
are true singers. Any man can write. . . ."
```

DIRECTIONS: Type the 2-page manuscript (a portion of a longer one) that follows. Use Procedure 1 (from LESSON 55) for typing footnotes on the *same* page where the reference appears. Type the quotation in proper form. Leave a 1-inch bottom margin. Include the page number at the top of your second page. Edit, proofread, and correct all errors. Remember—this manuscript will require 2 pages and you will have to follow the warning bell on your typewriter.

MARGINS: 6-inch line
DOUBLE SPACING

57-1   THE ORGANIZATION OF AMERICAN STATES

INTRODUCTION

     Latin America poses many problems to mankind today. This can be proven easily if one looks to recurrent social, economic, and political upheavals that plague our southern neighbors. Much must be done, therefore, to help improve the situation of life there so that there ~~is stable,~~ *are* productive, and progressive growth and *stable* government.

     The Organization of American States (~~hence-forth~~ *hereinafter* called OAS) was set up with the intention of dealing with the problems of ~~this~~ *the Western* hemisphere. ~~It appears that the~~ *There is a great* potential ~~of~~ *for* this organ~~ization~~ ~~is or may be the answer~~ to help Latin American develop properly. This paper will discuss the history of the OAS, its organization, its strengths and *its* weaknesses. It will try to analyze whether or not ~~the~~ *its* potential is being reached.

HISTORY

     Pan Americanism is often though*t* of as the Western Hemisphere Idea. It is this kind of thinking that probably was the basis for the interamerican system. According to this view:

(Problem 57-1 continued on next page.)

CHAPTER

III

LEARNING
NEW
SKILLS

LESSON

57

OBJECTIVE: To learn how to type a manuscript with headings and quotations.

DIRECTIONS: Type the warm-up line 3 times with <u>speed</u> as your goal.

MARGINS: 70-space line

TYPING A MANUSCRIPT WITH HEADINGS AND QUOTATIONS

YOU'RE ON THE HOMESTRETCH (45 WPM)!

GOAL: To type 45 or more wpm with no more than 1 error per minute.

WARM-UP

It was far too little too late to save the burning
building from loss.

Procedure for Typing Headings

MAIN HEADINGS:

These are capitalized and centered horizontally. Triple-space before and after.

SIDE HEADINGS:

These headings are typed at the left margin in FULL CAPS or <u>underscored.</u> Triple-space before and double-space after.

PARAGRAPH HEADINGS:

These are <u>underscored</u> and indented. Important words are capitalized. In general, these are treated as the regular beginning of a paragraph.

```
                                            3
                                    ← TRIPLE SPACE
_____
                                    ← TRIPLE SPACE
            MAIN HEADING
                                    ← TRIPLE SPACE
_____

                                    ← TRIPLE SPACE
SIDE HEADING                        ← DOUBLE SPACE
_____
_____
_____

    Paragraph Heading_____
_____
_____
```

Procedure for Typing Quotations

SHORT QUOTES:

These are run in with the text, typed with quotation marks before and after, and double-spaced. Generally, a short quote is considered no more than 2 sentences.

LONG QUOTES:

A long quote is generally *more* than 2 sentences or 2 typed lines. No quotation marks are used. The quote is ''set off'' from the text by moving the margins in 5 spaces on both sides and using single spacing. The first line of a paragraph within a long quote must have an additional indention of 5 spaces.

SHORT QUOTATION RUN
IN WITH TEXT

LONG QUOTATION SET OFF
(NO QUOTE MARKS)

WORD DIVISION AND USE OF THE DICTIONARY

WHEN IN DOUBT, CONSULT THE DICTIONARY.

GOAL: To type 21 or more wpm with no more than 1 error per minute.

OBJECTIVE: To practice dividing words properly.

DIRECTIONS: Type the warm-up line 3 times with <u>speed</u> as your goal.

MARGINS: 40-space line

WARM-UP

Put the car in the garage when you come.

RULES FOR WORD DIVISION

There are certain rules about word division you should know. They are shown below. If you are still in doubt, refer to a dictionary. Remember that you should not divide a word unless it is needed to make a more even right margin.

1. Not every word can be divided: for example, one-syllable words like *passed* or *helped*.
2. Use a dictionary to find correct syllables:
   prod/uct, *not* pro/duct
3. Never divide contractions or abbreviations:
   wouldn't, *not* would-n't
4. Leave at least the first 2 letters of a word on the first line and carry at least 3 letters of a word to the next line:
   al-though, *not* a-round;
   catch-ing, *not* catch-er
5. Never divide words at the ends of more than 2 successive typewritten lines.
6. If a vowel syllable stands alone in the body of a word, place it with the first syllable:
   busi-ness, *not* bus-iness

DIRECTIONS: Insert a sheet of paper into the typewriter and type the following list of 20 words, dividing them according to the rules just given. If you cannot divide the word, simply retype it as shown. Use double spacing. The key to this exercise follows.

21-1

1.	wouldn't	11.	tentatively
2.	advertise	12.	following
3.	kindly	13.	indent
4.	intersect	14.	divided
5.	answer	15.	amount
6.	checked	16.	summer
7.	product	17.	already
8.	eloped	18.	school
9.	paragraph	19.	foundation
10.	strength	20.	C.O.D.

SKILL IMPROVEMENT

DIRECTIONS: Type the accuracy and speed lines 3 times each. Take a 1-minute timing on each line, repeating copy as necessary. Then take a 1-minute timing on the control paragraph with 21 wpm as your goal. Be sure to indent 5 spaces before typing the first line.

MARGINS: 40-space line
SINGLE SPACING

Accuracy:

Mike was not able to get a fish for him.   8

Speed:

The boy should not go far out for rides.   8

Control Paragraph:

```
     Skill and experience will get you a      8
job but very often that is not enough to     16
enable you to hold it and progress; fre-     24
quently, the ability to work with people     32
of all types is considerably more impor-     40
tant to your success.                        44
```

| 1 | 2 | 3 | 4 | 5 | 6 | 7 | 8 |

The U. S. S. R. is also concerned. It has been
mentioned that rivers such as the Volga, the Ob,
the Yenisei, the Ural, and the Northern Dvina are
pol*luted* for substantial miles of their flows. In
fact, the Soviet public is increasingly alarmed
at the prospect of pollution of Lake Baikal since
this contains

10 percent of the world's fresh-water reserves. [4]

---

[1]Eric Pace, "Industrial Pollution--A Problem
for Some Dutch Tulip Growers," The New York Times
(March 1, 1970), p. 16.

[2]J. Weston Walch, Pollution Control--A Complete Handbook (Portland, Maine: J. Weston Walch,
1970), p. 62.

[3]Ibid., p. 59.

[4] *Marshall I. Goldman, editor, Controlling Pollution—
The Economics of a Cleaner America (Englewood Cliffs:
Prentice-Hall, Inc.), pp. 162—166.*

DIRECTIONS: Take a 1-minute timing on
the control paragraph, repeating copy
as necessary. Remember, your goal is to
type it at 44 wpm with no more than 1
error per minute.

MARGINS: 70-space line
SINGLE SPACING

SKILL IMPROVEMENT

(Refer to the Skill Improvement exercise in LESSON 36.)

	Word	Can it be Divided?	Reason
1.	wouldn't	No	Cannot divide contractions
2.	ad/ver/tise	Yes	Follows rules
3.	kind/ly (but)	No	Need three strokes on second line
	kind/ly. (and)	Yes	Follows rules
	kind/ly,	Yes	Follows rules
4.	in/ter/sect	Yes	Follows rules
5.	an/swer	Yes	Follows rules
6.	checked	No	Cannot divide one-syllable words
7.	prod/uct	Yes	Follows rules. Be sure syllables are correct. The division "pro/duct" is not correct.
8.	e/loped	No	Need two strokes on first line
9.	para/graph	Yes	Put single sounding syllable "a" on first line
10.	strength	No	Cannot divide one-syllable words
11.	ten/ta/tively	Yes	Divide at proper syllables. The "ly" cannot be divided unless a punctuation mark follows.
12.	fol/low/ing	Yes	Follows rules
13.	in/dent	Yes	Follows rules
14.	di/vi/ded	Yes	Follows rules
15.	a/mount	No	Need two strokes on first line
16.	sum/mer	Yes	Follows rules
17.	al/ready	Yes	Follows rules
18.	school	No	Cannot divide one-syllable words
19.	foun/da/tion	Yes	Follows rules
20.	C.O.D.	No	Cannot divide abbreviations

LESSON 56

OBJECTIVE: To practice typing a manuscript page with footnotes.

DIRECTIONS: Type the warm-up line 3 times with <u>control</u> as your goal.

MARGINS: 70-space line

DIRECTIONS: Type the 2-page manuscript (a portion of a longer one) that follows. Make all corrections as indicated. Use Procedure 1 (from LESSON 55) for typing footnotes. Type them in good form on the *same* page where the reference appears, leaving a 1-inch bottom margin. Edit, proofread, and correct all typing errors.

MARGINS: 60-space line
DOUBLE SPACING

TYPING AN EDITED MANUSCRIPT WITH FOOTNOTES

GOAL: To type 44 or more wpm with no more than 1 error per minute.

WARM-UP

The exciting experience was expected but we never realized the result.

56-1

INTERNATIONAL POLITICS AND POLLUTION

On many days one wonders how people live in some of our larger cities. The thick, dirty, polluted clouds that hang over some of them signal a concern that everyone should have ~~with~~ *about* the environment.

The cities in our country are not the only ones experiencing the problem. ~~The situation~~ *It* is shared by many cities in many countries all over the world. For example, dutch tulips are in jeopardy fo(r)m air pollution.[1] In Japan many people suffer from a smog-aggravated respiratory ailment which is known as the "Tokyo-Yokohama asthma." There have been times when oxygen tanks have been installed at busy Tokyo intersections for use by the traffic guards who must take an "oxygen break" every half hour.[2] East Germany has not escaped the problem either. It suffers from both air and water pollution and is trying to develop a system which would trap sulphur dioxide that comes from the chemical industries' smokestacks.[3]

(Problem 56-1 continued on next page.)

LESSON 22

OBJECTIVE: To learn to compute margins and to practice following the typewriter warning bell.

DIRECTIONS: Type the warm-up line 3 times with <u>accuracy</u> as your goal.

MARGINS: 40-space line

MARGIN THEORY AND FOLLOWING THE BELL

GOAL: To type 22 or more wpm with no more than 1 error per minute.

LISTEN FOR THE WARNING BELL.

WARM-UP

We are planning a trip to the mountains.

In computing margins, remember:

Size of paper
- The standard (USA) sheet of typing paper is 8 1/2″ by 11″ (21.5 cm by 28 cm). There are 66 lines available vertically on a full sheet (6 lines = 1″ or 2.5 cm).
- The metric sheet of typing paper is 21 cm by 29.7 cm. There are 70 lines available vertically on a full sheet.

Pitch
- For each horizontal inch or 2.5 cm, there are 10 spaces on a pica machine and 12 spaces on an elite machine.

Center Point
- On standard paper, the pica center will be 42 and the elite center will be 50.
- On metric paper, the pica center will be 42 and the elite center will be 50.

Procedure for Computing Margins

1. With the paper guide set at zero, insert the paper and find the center point of the paper.
2. Determine the length of the writing line you want. Whatever the length, half should be to the left of center, half to the right of center.

   On a pica machine, the margins for a centered *40-space line* are:

   22   42   62

   On an elite machine, the margins for a centered *60-space line* are:

   20   50   80

   Most typing assignments are done on a 40, 50, 60, or 70-space line.

3. In the instructions given in the remainder of this book you will be required to set margins for different length lines. Know what pitch you are using, see where the paper ends on the paper scale, and divide by 2.

Lesson 22: MARGIN THEORY AND FOLLOWING THE BELL   **28**

DIRECTIONS: Begin typing the last 2 lines of the body of the manuscript on line 52 of a full sheet of paper. Follow your bell and correct any errors. Then single-space and type the underscore 15 times. Double-space and type the footnote entry, indenting the first line. Single-space within the footnote. Again, be sure to follow the bell.

MARGINS: 60-space line

DIRECTIONS: Follow the same directions as in Problem 55-1, except to begin on line 42 of a full sheet of paper. Single-space within an entry but double-space between entries.

MARGINS: 60-space line

DIRECTIONS: Take a 1-minute timing on the control paragraph, repeating copy as necessary. Remember, your goal is to type it at 44 wpm with no more than 1 error per minute.

MARGINS: 70-space line
SINGLE SPACING

55-1

is being told this so that mistakes can be covered

up? What is the background of our energy problem?
_____

[1]"America's Energy Crisis," Newsweek, Vol. LXXI, No. 4 (January 22, 1973), p. 52.

55-2

primary energy is nothing more than new addi-

tions to energy. These are either of the per-
_____

[2]Chauncey Starr, "Energy and Power," Scientific American, Vol. 225, No. 3 (September, 1971), p. 37.

[3]Ibid.

[4]Raymond F. Dasmann, Environmental Conservation (New York: John Wiley & Sons, Inc., 1972), pp. 384–385.

SKILL IMPROVEMENT

(Refer to the Skill Improvement exercise in LESSON 35.)

A *60-space line* on a pica machine would be computed as follows:

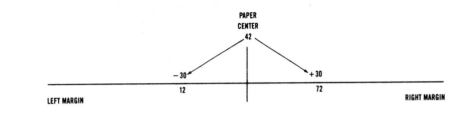

A *70-space line* on an elite machine would be computed as follows:

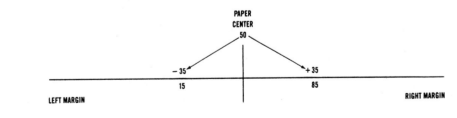

Following the Typewriter Bell

The TYPEWRITER BELL warns that you are approaching the right margin. When the bell rings, you must decide to:

- finish the word,
- divide the word, or
- type an additional word to even out the line.

In setting your margins, however, remember that you will want the warning bell to ring so that you may return to a new line without looking and also have even lines and margins. For this to be the case, always add a few extra spaces to your right margin so that the *bell* and not the margin stop will be at the end point of your writing line.

EXAMPLE:
For a 40-space line on a pica machine, you should set your left margin at 22 and have the bell ring at 62. Thus you would have to move your right margin stop to a point between 64 and 70 (depending on the machine) for the bell to ring at 62.

Left margin stop	40-space line	Bell rings at	Right margin stop
22		62	(Varies)

For practice, on a separate sheet of paper, compute margins for a 50-space line, a 70-space line, and a 5-inch line on both pica and elite typewriters.

REMEMBER: This is an easier method of typing footnotes. Be sure, however, to check which method is preferred.

Procedure 2—Typing Footnotes at the Back of the Manuscript

1. Center the word "Notes" on line 13. Type in full caps. Use a 60-space line and single spacing.
2. Triple-space after the heading.
3. Indent the first line of the note. Type the number on the line, followed by a period. Single-space within but double-space between notes.
4. Leave a 1-inch bottom margin.
5. On all other pages of notes, begin 3 spaces below the typed page number.
6. "Note" pages are part of the entire manuscript. Page numbers, therefore, must continue to be numbered consecutively.

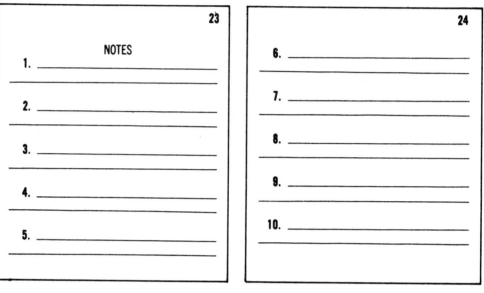

Procedure 3—Parenthetical Method of Typing Footnotes

Before using any method of typing footnotes, it is best to check on which is preferred by the school or the instructor.

A newer format is becoming acceptable. This is called the Parenthetical Method. They would be set up as follows:

- The name of the author or authors and page numbers are typed in parentheses following the information in the manuscript.
- Footnote numbers are not necessary.
- If there is more than one book by the same author, include publication date.
- Notes are not needed in the back.
- Bibliography MUST be typed.

> education. There seems to be a shortcoming, however, in
> the results we have obtained in our schools when measured
> against our own expectations and when comparisons are made
> to other countries like Japan (Clark, 392–394). It is
> hoped that some of these problems can be solved as we move
> into the last years of this century and the beginning of

DIRECTIONS: Set a 5-space tab indention. Then, following word division rules and listening for the bell, type this paragraph. The key to this exercise follows.

MARGINS: 70-space line
DOUBLE SPACING

DIRECTIONS: Set a 5-space tab indention. In typing this paragraph with the new margins, follow word division rules and listen for the bell. The key to this exercise follows.

MARGINS: 50-space line
DOUBLE SPACING

DIRECTIONS: Set a 5-space tab indention. Type this paragraph once, following word division rules and listening for the bell. Remember to even out your margins and your typed lines. The key to this exercise follows.

MARGINS: 5-inch line
DOUBLE SPACING

DIRECTIONS: Type the accuracy and speed lines 3 times each. Take a 1-minute timing on each line, repeating copy as necessary. Then take a 1-minute timing on the control paragraph with 22 wpm as your goal. Be sure to indent the first line 5 spaces.

MARGINS: 40-space line
SINGLE SPACING

22-1

It makes good sense to put important things first in all you do, and it is very important to do this when trying to improve your typing skill. There are many things that go into making you an expert typist, but the first is the use of the right techniques in each day's practice. Included in this is the efficient use of the working parts of the typewriter as well as stroking the keys with speed and control.

22-2

(Use the paragraph in Problem 22-1.)

22-3

Outdoor advertising is a big business. There is a great demand for billboard displays and special signs. When traveling on the highway, did you ever stop to consider who paid for the signs, who planned them, who designed them, and who considered the best place to put them? Yes, outdoor advertising is an exciting and excellent business.

SKILL IMPROVEMENT

Accuracy:
It takes time and hard work to type well.   8

Speed:
Try to be proud of your new typing skill.   8

Control Paragraph:
```
        What things do employers expect new      8
people to be able to do?  One of them is        16
trying to get the employees to be prompt        24
for work each morning.  Some of them may        32
require that workers be well dressed and        40
neat in all work they do.                       45
```

| 1 | 2 | 3 | 4 | 5 | 6 | 7 | 8 |

▶ *FOOTNOTE REFERENCE TO A NEWSPAPER[3]*

[3]Peter J. Nelson, "The Future Is Ours," <u>Philadelphia Gazette</u>, November 30, 1979, p. 14.

1. Author's name (or names) is written in natural order.
2. Title of article is placed in quotes. Name of paper is underscored. Volume number may be included but is not underscored.
3. Date is not placed in parentheses. Page number is last.

▶ *REPEATED FOOTNOTES[4]*

[4]<u>Ibid</u>.   or   [4]<u>Ibid</u>., pp. 333–334.   Means "in the same place as previously cited."

Procedure 1—Typing Footnotes at the Bottom of Each Page

1. Draw a warning line in light pencil 1 inch from the bottom of the paper.
2. Draw another warning line about 1 1/2 inches above the first warning line. In general, leave 1/2 inch for each footnote.
3. *On the first page:* type the title centered in caps on line 13.
   On all other pages: type the page number on line 7 at the right margin.
4. Return 3 times after the title or page number and begin or continue the manuscript. Begin each paragraph with a 5-space indention. Use a 60-space line.
5. Type the manuscript until you reach the first warning line. You must decide at this point whether you can type a few more lines or whether you should begin typing the footnotes.
6. Return once and type the underscore 15 times.
7. Return twice and begin typing the footnotes.
8. Indent the first line. Single-space within and double-space between. Be sure to leave a 1-inch bottom margin.

REMEMBER: Type only those footnotes for references that appear on the page. The last footnote should be typed so that there is a 1-inch bottom margin. Should the manuscript end in the middle of the page, the underscore line and footnote still are typed at the bottom, leaving a 1-inch margin, as illustrated below.

PAGE 1   **PAGE 2**   **PAGE 3**

(Underscore Line)

Double-space ⟶
Single-space ⟶
Double-space ⟶
Single-space ⟶

During this time his childhood was spent on a farm in Marceline, Missouri. His high school   } BODY

[1]Richard Schieckel, <u>The Disney Version</u> (New York: Simon and Schuster, 1968), p. 46.   } FOOTNOTE

22-1 KEY

70-space line
Margins 15 and 85 +
Elite machine

      It makes good sense to put important things first in all you do,

and it is very important to do this when trying to improve your typing

skill. There are many things that go into making you an expert typist,

but the first is the use of the right techniques in each day's practice.

Included in this is the efficient use of the working parts of the type-

writer as well as striking the keys with speed and control.

22-1 KEY

70-space line
Margins 7 and 77 +
Pica machine

    It makes good sense to put important things first in all you do,

and it is very important to do this when trying to improve your typing

skill. There are many things that go into making you an expert typist,

but the first is the use of the right techniques in each day's practice.

Included in this is the efficient use of the working parts of the type-

writer as well as striking the keys with speed and control.

LESSON

55

OBJECTIVE: To learn how to type footnotes.

DIRECTIONS: Type the warm-up line 3 times with <u>accuracy</u> as your goal.

MARGINS: 70-space line

TYPING FOOTNOTES

GOAL: To type 44 or more wpm with no more than 1 error per minute.

WARM-UP

When planning a party, first decide on your
guests; then choose the menu.

The purpose of footnotes is to add supplemental data to the text or to give credit to those whose information you used in preparing your paper. Any idea that is not your own—whether quoted directly or paraphrased—must be footnoted.

Such notes are called "footnotes" when they are typed at the foot of a page and "notes" when they are included at the back of the report or theme. If possible, footnote numbers in the text should follow the end of a sentence and any punctuation marks except a dash.

> *NOTE:* Footnote numbers in the text should be typed slightly ABOVE the line. Depending upon your typewriter, you may turn the cylinder by hand, use the VARIABLE LINE-SPACER, or use the RATCHET RELEASE. To use the ratchet release:
>
> ● Pull the ratchet release forward (toward you). Move the cylinder *away from you* about half a space.
> ● Type the raised number.
> ● Push back the ratchet release. Move the cylinder *towards you* until you feel the "click."
>
> Footnote numbers at the bottom of the page either may be typed slightly above the line or, a more common practice today, may be typed on the line and followed by a period.

Here are examples of several types of footnotes:

▶ *FOOTNOTE REFERENCE TO A BOOK[1]*

> [1]John C. Smith and Richard Deene, <u>How To Study</u> (New
> York: Sullivan Book Company, 1978), p. 3.

1. Author's name (or names) is written in natural order.
2. Title of book is underscored.
3. Place of publication, name of publisher, and date of publication are placed in parentheses.
4. Use small "p." or "pp." for *page* or *pages* followed by the number and a period.
5. All parts of footnotes are separated by commas, except before a parenthesis.

▶ *FOOTNOTE REFERENCE TO A MAGAZINE OR PERIODICAL[2]*

> 2. Karen Mason, "Back to Basics," <u>Education</u>, XV (May,
> 1979), pp. 16–17.

1. Author's name (or names) is written in natural order.
2. Title of article is placed in quotes.
3. Title of publication is underscored. Do not underscore volume number.
4. Date of publication is placed in parentheses and followed by page number.

It makes good sense to put important things first in all you do, and it is very important to do this when trying to improve your typing skill. There are many things that go into making you an expert typist, but the first is the use of the right techniques in each day's practice. Included in this is the efficient use of the working parts of the typewriter as well as striking the keys with speed and control.

It makes good sense to put important things first in all you do, and it is very important to do this when trying to improve your typing skill. There are many things that go into making you an expert typist, but the first is the use of the right techniques in each day's practice. Included in this is the efficient use of the working parts of the typewriter as well as striking the keys with speed and control.

DIRECTIONS: Type the following sales report in good form. Begin the title on line 13, spread-centering it (you may need 2 lines); then triple-space before starting to type the report. You will need a second page. Proofread carefully and correct all errors.

MARGINS: 6-inch line
DOUBLE SPACING

SALES REPORT FOR THE MONTH OF MARCH 1988

It is a pleasure to write that our sales for the past month have increased by 5 percent overall. We have had tremendous support from branch managers in their efforts to inspire all employees involved with our products to double and triple their efforts in pushing sales.

The two products that showed the most potential and, in fact, had the most increase in sales were QUICK GLUE and FIX-IT-UP. The volume of both these products was increased by more than 10 percent resulting from a new ad campaign supported by new jingles and appropriate photography that was "catchy" to the public's eye.

It has been decided by management to determine the potential for a new art paste (name for product not yet approved) that would greatly aid those artists involved in layout designs. Although the products on the market at the present time are most satisfactory, we feel that we have the ability to produce a better one that would be able to meet *and beat* the competition.

We are also interested in investigating the possibility of a new frame glue that would be superior to the one we are now marketing for wooden frames. As of now, we plan to have this on the agenda of next month's divisional meetings to be held in New York, Chicago, Denver, and Los Angeles.

With regard to those products that showed the least increase in sales--namely, YELLOW PASTE and EZY--we hope that we can improve this situation in the next month. If these products continue to decline, we will have to determine the problems involved and whether improvements in the products or their advertising are needed.

As always, we thank all our employees for the role they have played in making our products the best and for helping to give us the reputation for excellence that we have in the art supply industry.

DIRECTIONS: Take a 1-minute timing on the control paragraph, repeating copy as necessary. Remember, your goal is to type it at 44 wpm with no more than 1 error per minute.

MARGINS: 70-space line
SINGLE SPACING

SKILL IMPROVEMENT

(Refer to the Skill Improvement exercise in LESSON 34.)

Outdoor advertising is a big business. There is a great
demand for billboard displays and special signs. When traveling on the highway, did you ever stop to consider who paid for
the signs, who planned them, who designed them, and who considered the best place to put them? Yes, outdoor advertising
is an exciting and excellent business.

Outdoor advertising is a big business. There is
a great demand for billboard displays and special signs.
When traveling on the highway, did you ever stop to
consider who paid for the signs, who planned them, who
designed them, and who considered the best place to
put them? Yes, outdoor advertising is an exciting and
excellent business.

DIRECTIONS: Type in good form the following rough draft of a theme. Make all corrections as indicated. Begin the title on line 13, triple-space after the spread-centered title, and double-space the body of the manuscript. Use a second page. Proofread carefully and correct all errors.

MARGINS: 6-inch line
DOUBLE SPACING

REMEMBER: Be sure to insert and check for the warning line.

O U R   P O L I T I C A L   W O R L D

Who is to say that our political world today is any worse or better than 20, 30, or even 40 years ago? On the television and radio we can now get all the news very quickly about the candidates, their views, their goals, and their past histories. We can see them in action on a day-to-day basis.

In the past the public had to rely basically on newspapers to bring it up to date on the events that surrounded political activity. People now--as in the past--are weary and tired of listening to all the promises only to find that they are broken soon after the person is elected to office.

Now as before there have always existed the political maneuverings of power in smoke-filled hotel rooms and convention halls. There were "dark horses" then, and there are "dark horses" now. These are people who come to power (by staying in the background) when decisions about regular candidates can not be made. They wait in the "wings" of the convention hall for the moment when they are called to enter the "arena." The people don't really have a say in this. Is this fair?

Perhaps it isn't fair, but this is the way it is. At least this is the way it is until it can be changed. But who is going to change it? Many believe that our system has worked, and it is still working. What do you think?

You must let your elected officials know exactly where you stand. In our democracy they work for you. Don't be shy! Write them or visit them. Tell them what you think. That <u>can</u> bring change.

LESSON

23

OBJECTIVE: To learn to type from handwritten copy.

DIRECTIONS: Type the warm-up line 3 times with <u>control</u> as your goal.

MARGINS: 40-space line

INTRODUCTION TO HANDWRITTEN COPY

LOOK AT THE COPY, NOT THE KEYBOARD

GOAL: To type 23 or more wpm with no more than 1 error per minute.

WARM-UP

Jeff wrote an excellent paper on travel.

Procedure for Typing from Handwritten Copy

- Even out the right and left margins. Even out the line endings. No line should be more than 4 spaces off.
- Avoid dividing words if possible. If you must divide, then follow word division rules, using a dictionary to be sure you are dividing properly.
- Your typed lines will not follow exactly or be the same length as your handwritten lines. They will follow the margins you have set and the warning bell near the end of the line.

Note the difference between the following handwritten copy and the typed 50-space-line copy.

Spring is a beautiful season of the year. The birds chirp, the flowers grow, and the grass is green. It is a beautiful season of the year. It is the time of year when a young man's fancy turns to love.

        Spring is a beautiful season of the year. The
birds chirp, the flowers grow, and the grass is
green. It is a beautiful season of the year. It
is the time of year when a young man's fancy turns
to love.

DIRECTIONS: Type the handwritten copy indicated, using a 5-space tab indention. When you are finished, circle your errors and fold your paper in half lengthwise to see that no line is more than 4 spaces off from the other. Are your margins as even as possible?

MARGINS: 40-space line
DOUBLE SPACING

23-1

(Use the handwritten copy in the above example.)

DIRECTIONS: Type the following hand-written paragraph, using a 5-space tab indention.

MARGINS: 60-space line
DOUBLE SPACING

23-2

When you are efficient in the way you plan your study schedule, studying tends to be easier. You will also find that you obtain better results from study that is planned and organized. Begin today to plan your study time. The benefits will be many, and you will be pleased with how easy studying can be.

PREPARING A SIMPLE THEME OR REPORT

A WARNING LINE SAVES TIME!

GOAL: To type 44 or more wpm with no more than 1 error per minute.

OBJECTIVE: To learn the correct procedure for typing a simple theme or report.

DIRECTIONS: Type the warm-up line 3 times with <u>speed</u> as your goal.

MARGINS: 70-space line

THE PAGE NUMBER is not generally typed on the first page.

WARM-UP

It is easy to plan but sometimes hard to carry out our daily projects.

Procedure for Typing a Simple Theme or Report

▶ *FIRST PAGE*

1. Set margins for a 6-inch line (60 spaces/pica, 72 spaces/elite). Set a tab for a 5-space indention.
2. Place a light pencil line (about 1 inch long) at the left margin an inch from the bottom of the paper (the warning line).
3. Center the title of the theme or report on line 13. Type in full CAPS. Triple-space before starting the body of the theme.
4. Set the line-space regulator for double spacing and begin typing the manuscript. Remember to check for the warning line.

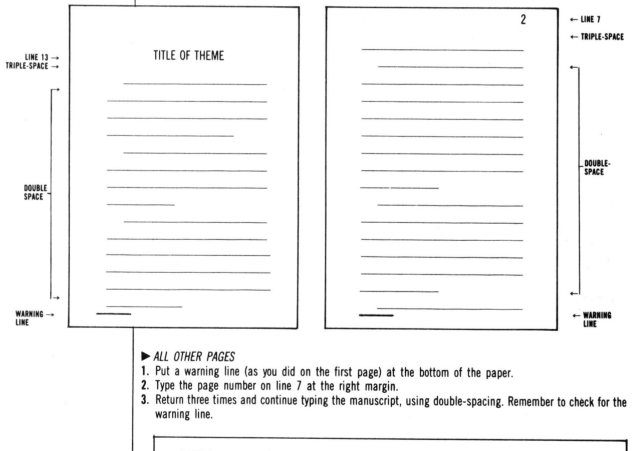

LINE 13 →
TRIPLE-SPACE →

TITLE OF THEME

DOUBLE SPACE

WARNING → LINE

2   ← LINE 7
← TRIPLE-SPACE

DOUBLE-SPACE

← WARNING LINE

▶ *ALL OTHER PAGES*

1. Put a warning line (as you did on the first page) at the bottom of the paper.
2. Type the page number on line 7 at the right margin.
3. Return three times and continue typing the manuscript, using double-spacing. Remember to check for the warning line.

> *NOTE:* In general, a 6-inch line (60 spaces on pica and 72 spaces on elite) is used for manuscript work. If, however, the material is to be bound, move your left margin in an additional 5 spaces to leave room for binding.

DIRECTIONS: Type the following hand-written paragraph, using a 5-space tab indention:

MARGINS: 50-space line
DOUBLE SPACING

REMEMBER, to construct the exclamation point
    Type apostrophe '
    Backspace
    Type period :
Leave 2 spaces after an exclamation point.

DIRECTIONS: Type the following hand-written paragraph once, using a 5-space tab indention. Proofread by circling errors. Try it a second time if you have made more than three errors.

MARGINS: 60-space line
DOUBLE SPACING

DIRECTIONS: Type the accuracy and speed lines 3 times each. Take a 1-minute timing on each line, repeating copy as necessary. Then take a 1-minute timing on the control paragraph with 23 wpm as your goal. Indent the first line 5 spaces.

MARGINS: 40-space line
SINGLE SPACING

23-3

We have a beautiful country! The scenery is so varied and pleasant that the traveler cannot help but marvel at what he sees. The mountains of the far West, the plains of the Midwest, and the rolling hills of the East are unequaled anywhere. If you ever get the opportunity to travel across the United States — whether by car, bus, or train — do it! You will never forget your journey. You will be proud of your country.

23-4

History is an important subject to study and understand. It has been said that a generation is bound to commit the same errors unless they understand the mistakes of the past.

There are several instances where history has repeated itself. Didn't World War II come after World War I? Didn't our defeat in Vietnam follow twenty years after the defeat of the French in Indochina?

SKILL IMPROVEMENT

Accuracy:

```
The firm held the title to the property.    8
```

Speed:

```
The skill of the typist is easy to gain.    8
```

Control Paragraph:

```
     When you type, think of each of the    8
words in the line.  The way to improve a   16
skill such as typing is to put forth the   24
effort necessary to reach a stated goal.   32
You will soon be able to see some steady   40
progress as you continue to work.          47
```

```
|  1  |  2  |  3  |  4  |  5  |  6  |  7  |  8  |
```

DIRECTIONS: Type an exact copy of the following table of contents. Use a 60-space line for horizontal placement and center the table vertically on a full sheet of paper. Be sure that all leaders are aligned.

MARGINS: 60-space line
DOUBLE SPACING

53-1

TABLE OF CONTENTS

DIRECTIONS: Type an exact copy of the following table of contents. Use a 60-space line for horizontal placement and center the material vertically on a full sheet of paper. Erase and correct all errors. Be sure to center horizontally EACH unit number and title in this problem.

MARGINS: 60-space line
SINGLE SPACING

53-2

TABLE OF CONTENTS

DIRECTIONS: Take a 1-minute timing on the control paragraph, repeating copy as necessary. Remember, your goal is to type it at 44 wpm with no more than 1 error per minute.

MARGINS: 70-space line
SINGLE SPACING

SKILL IMPROVEMENT

(Refer to the Skill Improvement exercise in LESSON 33.)

LESSON 24

TYPING FROM PROOFREADERS' SYMBOLS AND EDITED COPY

GOAL: To type 24 or more wpm with no more than 1 error per minute.

OBJECTIVE: To learn common proofreaders' symbols and to develop your ability to type from rough draft copy.

DIRECTIONS: Type the warm-up line 3 times with <u>speed</u> as your goal.

MARGINS: 40-space line

WARM-UP

Our club will send you a gift in a week.

It is frequently necessary to revise something that has been typewritten. The original copy is called a *rough draft*. Markings or symbols used by writers, editors, and typists to indicate such changes are called proofreaders' symbols. Some of the most common ones are illustrated here:

∧ = insert	# = space	/ = Change Letter
ℐ = delete	⌒ = close up space	
ℓ.c. = lowercase letters	⁋ = paragraph	·········· = Keep in Material Originally Deleted
∪ = transpose	no ⁋ = no paragraph	
⌐ = move to right; indent	⌐ = move to left	

The following example shows how three lines of rough draft material with handwritten corrections may appear.

⑤ Rough drafts are gen*ℓ*rally double-spaced that
the wri*ø*er has sufficient space on the copy to insert ~~the~~
handwritten correc(ti)ons with out difficulty.

Correctly typed, the example would look like this:

        Rough drafts are generally double-spaced so
    that the writer has sufficient space on the copy
    to insert handwritten corrections without diffi-
    culty.

24-1

DIRECTIONS: Retype this rough draft, making all the corrections indicated. Follow the warning bell.

MARGINS: 50-space line
DOUBLE SPACING

        The way you solve problems is very important.
    Instead of trying (bring/to) things back to normal
    when difficulties/arise, you should take advantage
    of disaster to create something better ~~than you~~
    th*a*n that with which you started. ⁋Discipline is
    a n impro/tant part/of solving problems. You must
    work, work, and work some more, to get where you
    are ~~heading~~

LESSON

53

OBJECTIVE: To learn how to prepare a table of contents.

DIRECTIONS: Type the warm-up line 3 times with <u>control</u> as your goal.

MARGINS: 70-space line

PREPARING A TABLE OF CONTENTS

GOAL: To type 44 or more wpm with no more than 1 error per minute.

WARM-UP

In the town we saw people enjoying the holiday by
attending a concert.

Procedure for Typing a Table of Contents

- Use a 60-space line. Center vertically. Line-space according to the style of contents desired. Triple-space after centering the words TABLE OF CONTENTS.
- Type the word "Chapter" or "Part" at the left margin. Center and align the chapter or part numbers under it. "Pivot" the word "page" from the right margin (see the explanation of "pivoting" in the *Note* below), and align the page numbers under it, as shown in the illustration in Problem 53-1.
- Align the *leaders* (row of dots) correctly. The last leader in each line should end approximately 4 spaces before the page number.

To align leaders correctly, note the following procedure:

- Type the first leader 2 spaces after the last word on a line. Determine whether it has been typed at an odd or even point on your paper scale.
- All additional leaders should be consistent with the first one. In cases where one line is odd and another even, start your leaders 3 spaces after the last word typed. NEVER type a leader in the very first space after the last word on a line.
- Type the leaders by alternating the period and the space bar.

NOTE: To PIVOT means to "justify" or to align at the right margin the last letters of words typed.

EXAMPLE:

shown|
man|
guards|

TO PIVOT:
1. Move to *one space beyond the point* you wish the item you are aligning to end.
2. Backspace for *each* letter and each space.
3. Type the item. It will end where you wish.

EXAMPLES:

A. Suppose you want the heading "Page 2" to end exactly at the right margin:

1. Move to one space beyond the margin.
2. Backspace once for *P*
    once for *a*
    once for *g*
    once for *e*
    once for *space*
    once for *2*
3. Type "Page 2." It will end at the margin.   Page 2|

```
x|  = Margin
 |x = One space
      beyond
```

B. Suppose you want to pivot the date, *September 1, 1984:*

1. Move to one space beyond the margin.
2. Backspace once for each space in the date.
3. When backspacing is completed, type the date. It should end exactly at the right margin.

DIRECTIONS: Retype this rough draft, making all the corrections indicated. Follow the warning bell.

MARGINS: 50-space line
DOUBLE SPACING

Editing rough drafts is a very important aspect of keyboarding. This means it will be necessary to use proofreading marks and editing notations before doing the final draft. There will be other times when several drafts will be necessary before you are satisfied. Aim for perfection in Grammar, spelling, punctuation, sentence structure and the organization of your ideas.

Editing is an important part of preparing the final draft. Do it as clearly and concisely as possible.

DIRECTIONS: Type the accuracy and speed lines 3 times each. Take a 1-minute timing on each line, repeating copy as necessary. Then take a 1-minute timing on the control paragraph with 24 wpm as your goal. Indent the first line 5 spaces.

MARGINS: 40-space line
SINGLE SPACING

SKILL IMPROVEMENT

Accuracy:

```
Now is the time for me to build my skill.    8
```

Speed:

```
My goal is to try to get a very good job.    8
```

Control Paragraph:

```
        You do not have to raise your voice     8
to be heard.  You should always remember       16
to try to speak slowly.  One of the best       24
ways to be heard is first to be a better       32
listener.  The person who is speaking is       40
going to notice that you are very polite.      48
```

```
|  1  |  2  |  3  |  4  |  5  |  6  |  7  |  8  |
```

TOURING BIG CITIES

DIRECTIONS: Set up the following handwritten outline in good form. Center it vertically and horizontally on a full sheet of paper. Proofread and correct your errors.

NOTE: Some handwritten lines may look longer than others but in reality are not. Double check by counting similar looking lines just to be sure the Key Line will be accurate.

DIRECTIONS: Take a 1-minute timing on the control paragraph, repeating copy as necessary. Remember, your goal is to type it at 43 wpm with no more than 1 error per minute.

MARGINS: 70-space line
SINGLE SPACING

I. ORGANIZED TOURS
   A. Special tours given by private companies
      1. Bus
      2. Boat
   B. Organized walking tours
      1. Special streets
      2. Historic neighborhoods
      3. Famous houses
         a. Birthplaces of important people

II. INDIVIDUAL TOURS
   A. Via public transportation
      1. Bus
      2. Streetcar
      3. Subway (metro)
   B. Walking
      1. Using a map denoting special points of interest
      2. Strolling at random
         a. Surprise turns

SKILL IMPROVEMENT

(Refer to the Skill Improvement exercise in LESSON 32.)

COMPOSING AT THE TYPEWRITER

GOAL: To type 25 or more wpm with no more than 1 error per minute.

OBJECTIVE: To practice composing at the typewriter.

DIRECTIONS: Type the warm-up line 3 times with <u>accuracy</u> as your goal.

MARGINS: 40-space line

DIRECTIONS: Compose answers to the following questions. Write the answers in complete sentences. Choose the length of your writing line and the line spacing.

REMEMBER: You should not look at your fingers while you are composing, but at the paper in the typewriter.

DIRECTIONS: Compose two simple sentences about each of these topics. Choose the margins and line spacing.

DIRECTIONS: Compose a simple paragraph on the following subject. Use a 5-space tab indention.

MARGINS: 50-space line
DOUBLE SPACING

DIRECTIONS: Type the accuracy and speed lines 3 times each. Take a 1-minute timing on each line, repeating copy as necessary. Then take a 1-minute timing on the control paragraph with 25 wpm as your goal. Indent the first line 5 spaces.

MARGINS: 40-space line
SINGLE SPACING

WARM-UP

He told me I should not change my plans.

25-1

What is your name?
What is today's date?
What is the name of your school or company?

25-2

Sports
Vacation
My Future Plans

25-3

A description of the plot of a recent movie

SKILL IMPROVEMENT

Accuracy:
Bill was unable to move the carton away.   8

Speed:
Perhaps he was not willing to try again.   8

Control Paragraph:
     A voice that is clear is easy to be   8
heard. How you talk will get results if   16
you try to be convincing when it is your   24
turn to speak. Until that time, you can   32
keep happy by just being a good listener   40
You might have heard that listening will   48
require more effort on your part.   56

| 1 | 2 | 3 | 4 | 5 | 6 | 7 | 8 |

DIRECTIONS: Make a copy of the following outline. Center it vertically and horizontally. Proofread, and correct your errors.

52-1

LEFT MARGIN   TAB   TAB   TYPING AN OUTLINE

↓3

   I. HORIZONTAL PLACEMENT

↓2

      A. Clear all margins and tabs.
      B. Center Key Line
          1. Backspace once for every two spaces   [KEY LINE ENDS]
              from point farthest left to point
              farthest right
          2. Set tabs

↓3

[KEY LINE BEGINS →]   II. VERTICAL PLACEMENT

↓2

      A. Compute using Hush Method
      B. Spacing and Headings
          1. Triple space after Main Title
          2. Triple space before main heading
               and double space after it.
          3. Type main headings in caps.

DIRECTIONS: Make a copy of the following outline. Center it vertically and horizontally. Proofread, and correct your errors.

52-2

LEFT MARGIN   TAB   TAB   TAB   BEST METHODS OF STUDY

   I. LOCATION

↓2

      A. Find a quiet place
          1. Preferably away from other members   [KEY LINE ENDS]
              of the family
          2. Near sources of reference
      B. Avoid distractions
          1. Radio
          2. Television
          3. Telephone

↓3

  II. STUDY SCHEDULE

↓2

      A. Plan assignments
          1. Cover most difficult assignments
              first
          2. Spread homework out into 40-minute
              segments
          a. Take a short break after each
              segment

↓3

[KEY LINE BEGINS →]   III. STUDY TECHNIQUES

↓2

      A. Underlining
          1. Use felt pens to cover lines
          2. Be neat
      B. Outlining
      C. Memorizing
      D. Use association

LESSON

26

OBJECTIVE: To practice editing a portion of a newspaper article.

DIRECTIONS: Type the warm-up line 3 times with <u>control</u> as your goal.

MARGINS: 50-space line

DIRECTIONS: This is a rough draft of a portion of a news article. Edit the copy to the best of your ability and then retype it from the edited copy. Be sure to use the proofreader's symbols you previously learned. Check your work by referring to the corrected copy, which is shown at the end of the next lesson (27).

MARGINS: 50-space line
DOUBLE SPACING

DIRECTIONS: Type the accuracy and speed lines 3 times each. Take a 1-minute timing on each line, repeating copy as necessary. Then take a 1-minute timing on the control paragraph with 26 wpm as your goal. Indent the first line 5 spaces.

MARGINS: 50-space line
SINGLE SPACING

EDITING COMPOSED COPY

GOAL: to type 26 or more wpm with no more than 1 error per minute.

WARM-UP

Be sure to remain very quiet while in the library.

Procedure for Editing

- Use either a pencil or pen.
- Using proofreader's symbols (see LESSON 24), mark corrections in spelling, punctuation, word choice, or arrangement.

26-1

      The annaul senior awards Program will take
place in the auditorimm of the high school on Wed.
Jun. 4th, at 8 p.m.

      This program to which all seniors and thier
parents are invited is presented to honur the young
men and woman of this high school for their scho-
larstic achievements. Scholarships will be awarded
and awards for atheletes will also be distributed
out.

      The high school orchestra will play selections
at the begining and end of the programm.

SKILL IMPROVEMENT

Accuracy:
Ask him for an easy way to move toward your goals. 10

Speed:
Make up simple rules and you will be able to lead. 10

Control Paragraph

    The more she types, the faster she will learn 10
to type. She will soon be a rapid typist and may 20
be able to put this valuable skill to use in quite 30
a number of personal and business tasks. One time 40
soon she will be able to reap the rewards and then 50
the effort to persevere will be worthwhile.   58

| 1 | 2 | 3 | 4 | 5 | 6 | 7 | 8 | 9 | 10 |

LESSON

52

OBJECTIVE: To learn how to prepare an outline.

DIRECTIONS: Type the warm-up line 3 times with <u>accuracy</u> as your goal.

MARGINS: 70-space line

PREPARING AN OUTLINE

GOAL: To type 43 or more wpm with no more than 1 error per minute.

WARM-UP

```
Four girls in the playground seemed to enjoy
themselves on the swings.
```

Procedure for Preparing a Typewritten Outline

● Center the KEY LINE (the total number of spaces used from left to right) *horizontally*.
● Center the outline *vertically*, including the title.
● Triple-space after the title and before each main subdivision. Double-space after each main subdivision. Single-space all other parts.
● Indent each segment of the outline 4 spaces and set a tab at these points. Each segment number or letter is followed by a period and 2 spaces. Align numbers and letters. Long lines are divided, with the second part beginning under the first word of the first part. (See item 1 under "A" in the outline in Problem 52-1.)

NOTE: When typing roman numerals, keep in mind the following:

1. Use capital letters. For number 1, use capital I.

    I = 1   V = 5   X = 10   L = 50
    C = 100   D = 500   M = 1,000

2. Align roman numerals on the RIGHT.

       I.   IV.   VII.
      II.   V.   VIII.
     III.   VI.   IX.

3. Always type a period (.) after the roman numeral in a listing.

LESSON 27

OBJECTIVE: To learn to use proper correcting techniques on typewritten work.

DIRECTIONS: Type the warm-up line 3 times with <u>speed</u> as your goal.

MARGINS: 50-space line.

DIRECTIONS: Insert a sheet of paper into the typewriter and type the following sentences. Then correct each one according to the directions given.

MARGINS: 60-space line
DOUBLE SPACING

DIRECTIONS: Correct any errors you make as you type the following paragraph:

MARGINS: 50-space line
DOUBLE SPACING

CORRECTING TECHNIQUES

GOAL: To type 27 or more wpm with no more than 1 error per minute.

DON'T STRIKE OVER AN ERROR.

WARM-UP

Travel can be a very happy way to spend your time.

In making corrections, you may use a special typewriter eraser, Ko-Rec-Type, or white correction fluid, or you may have a typewriter equipped with a correcting cartridge or other correcting mechanism. It is necessary, therefore, to familiarize yourself with the typewriter you are using to determine the most efficient correcting technique.

27-1

	Change	To
1. I saw the books over three.	three	there
2. Our class will meet at the arene at 3 p.m.	arene	arena
3. Pennsylvania is known as the keystone State.	keystone	Keystone
4. The red maple tree has lsot its leaves.	lsot	lost
5. Please stay in the seet assigned.	seet	seat

27-2

There will be little change in temperature today as warm, humid weather remains over our area of the country. The only chance of relief is the prospect of late afternoon or early evening thundershowers. The forecast for the rest of the week holds some hope for relief from the heat wave. It will cool gradually as a cool front approaches from the west.

Here is the corrected copy of the problem in LESSON 26:

The annual senior Awards Program will take place in the auditorium of the high school on Wednesday, June 4, at 8 p.m.

This program, to which all seniors and their parents are invited, is presented to honor the young men and women of this high school for their scholastic achievements. Scholarships will be awarded, and awards for athletes will also be distributed.

The high school orchestra will play selections at the beginning and end of the program.

CHAPTER

VIII

TYPING
MANUSCRIPTS

DIRECTIONS: Type the accuracy and speed lines 3 times each. Take a 1-minute timing on each line, repeating copy as necessary. Then take a 1-minute timing on the control paragraph with 27 wpm as your goal. Indent the first line 5 spaces.

MARGINS: 50-space line
SINGLE SPACING

SKILL IMPROVEMENT

Accuracy:
To type well all you need is a desire to practice.   10

Speed:
Do all work right the first time to achieve goals.   10

Control Paragraph:

      Oral and written skills are important to your   10
success on the job. In addition, you will need to   20
sharpen your human relations skills so that no one   30
will find fault with you. Remember this point for   40
gaining success in life. Remember, too, that your   50
smile can go a long way to insure your success.   60

| 1 | 2 | 3 | 4 | 5 | 6 | 7 | 8 | 9 | 10 |

LESSON 51

COMPOSING AND EDITING PERSONAL BUSINESS LETTERS

COPY ALWAYS AT THE RIGHT

GOAL: To type 43 or more wpm with no more than 1 error per minute.

OBJECTIVE: Given a situation, to compose, edit, revise, and retype the letter in good form.

DIRECTIONS: To type the warm-up line 3 times with _speed_ as your goal.

MARGINS: 70-space line

DIRECTIONS: Read the following situation. Then compose a rough draft for a letter of response. Follow good composition techniques. Use a 5-space tab paragraph indention.

MARGINS: 60-space line
DOUBLE SPACING

DIRECTIONS: Using the proofreader's symbols you learned in **LESSON 24**, revise your draft with a pencil or pen. Make any additions, deletions, or changes you think necessary. Prepare your edited copy so that it will be easy to follow when typing the final copy.

DIRECTIONS: Using the following address, type the final copy of the rough draft you have just edited. Use semi-blocked style and mixed punctuation. Prepare a carbon and an envelope. Type in good form, correcting all errors neatly. Don't forget to include your return address in the heading and your typed and written signature at the end of the letter. Fold the original and insert it into an envelope.

MARGINS: 60-space line
SINGLE SPACING

DIRECTIONS: Take a 1-minute timing on the control paragraph, repeating copy as necessary. Remember, your goal is to type it at 43 wpm with no more than 1 error per minute.

MARGINS: 70-space line
SINGLE SPACING

WARM-UP

Over the river and through the wood to the house
of grandmother we go.

51-1

THE SITUATION: You have recently read a newspaper editorial that favors the closing of two hospitals in the area. However, the buildings are in good shape, and there is a realistic and positive need for their staying in operation.

Although the main argument for closing the hospital is cost, you think differently. For example, what will the patients in the area do for emergency services? How about the poor people? Will they be able to afford the expense of traveling out of the area for their medical services? What about the present overcrowding in other hospitals? How will closing these hospitals alleviate that problem?

You simply don't agree with the editorial—in fact, you are almost angry about it. How can your letter influence the newspaper to change its opinion?

COMPOSITION: Let this newspaper know what you think. Express your opinion. Try to keep the letter to three short paragraphs.

51-2

(Use the rough draft from Problem 51-1.)

51-3

The Daily Telegram / Office of the Editor in Chief /
2 Main Street / Your City, State and Zip Code

SKILL IMPROVEMENT

(Refer to the Skill Improvement exercise in LESSON 31.)

CROWDING TECHNIQUES

GOAL: To type 28 or more wpm with no more than 1 error per minute.

TAKE PRIDE IN YOUR TYPING.

OBJECTIVE: To learn how to crowd letters on the writing line when it is necessary to do so.

DIRECTIONS: Type the warm-up line 3 times with <u>accuracy</u> as your goal.

MARGINS: 50-space line

WARM-UP

All of our flowers are beginning to bloom at once.

On a piece of paper type the following sentence as shown:

We have been unable to chek its validity.

It is necessary to insert (or "crowd") an extra "c" in "chek" to avoid erasing the rest of the line.

In order to crowd, you must move all letters in the word a half space closer. The method you will use to half-space will depend upon the mechanics of your particular typewriter.

- If your typewriter has a *half-space key*, press and hold it down before each stroke. On some typewriters the space bar can be held down to half-space the carriage.
- OR, using the *backspace key*, before each stroke press and hold down the key at approximately half-down depth.
- OR, before each stroke, press against the left end of the carriage, pushing it back a half space and holding it in place while you strike the key.

Having determined which method of carriage control you will use, you are now ready to retype the incorrect word "chek."

REMEMBER: *If you are <u>crowding</u> letters, you will need to move less than a full space for each letter. This procedure takes patience, practice, and judgment. Your goal is to make corrections of this nature in such a way that they will not be noticed from the regularly spaced typing of other words.*

Procedure for Crowding

1. Erase the letter before the error *(h)*, the error itself *(ek)*, and the letter after the error (in this case, there is a space).
2. Manually move the carriage or carriage-element component into the spaces where the new letters will be typed.
3. Using one of the methods of carriage control just mentioned, fill in the missing letters. Keep your eye on the print-point indicator when judging where to place the letters.

DIRECTIONS: Type each of these sentences as you see them **WITH THE ERROR.** Following the directions on each line, erase and crowd to make the correction indicated:

MARGINS: 55-space line
DOUBLE SPACING

28-1

	Change	To
1. Coal miners are a very study group.	study	sturdy
2. He takes too muchfor granted.	muchfor	much for
3. Monthly meetings are hld by the Club.	hld	held
4. This is our third request for action.	third	second
5. The data was highly inaccurate.	was	were

LESSON

50

OBJECTIVE: To practice composing personal business letters, using guided paragraphs.

DIRECTIONS: Type the warm-up line 3 times with <u>control</u> as your goal.

MARGINS: 70-space line

DIRECTIONS: Compose a personal business letter on the typewriter, using the following guided paragraphs. Save this rough draft; you will need it to complete the additional problems in this lesson.

MARGINS: 60-space line
DOUBLE SPACING

DIRECTIONS: Using the proofreaders' symbols you learned in LESSON 24, revise your draft with a pencil or pen.

DIRECTIONS: Type the letter in final form with 1 copy, using the address shown. Use blocked style and mixed punctuation. Correct all errors and prepare an envelope.

MARGINS: 60-space line
SINGLE SPACING

DIRECTIONS: Take a 1-minute timing on the control paragraph, repeating copy as necessary. Remember, your goal is to type it at 43 wpm with no more than 1 error per minute.

MARGINS: 70-space line
SINGLE SPACING

COMPOSING PERSONAL BUSINESS LETTERS

GOAL: To type 43 or more wpm with no more than 1 error per minute.

WARM-UP

An agency delivered the letter directly to the other side of the city.

When composing, keep in mind the following:

● Keep your eyes on the paper in the typewriter. Keep the machine going in order to get your thoughts down on paper. You can revise later.
● Use a 60-space line, double spacing, and a 5-space tab indention.
● You may x out all errors.

50-1

THE SITUATION: You and your family are planning to take a trip to the New England area this summer. Therefore you are to write a letter to the Chamber of Commerce in New Hampshire for information that might be helpful for tourists in planning their trip.

    Paragraph 1: Inform the Chamber of Commerce that you and your family are planning a trip to New Hampshire during the month of July and that you would like information they think might be helpful.

    Paragraph 2: The kind of information you want would be that which deals with roads, inns and hotels, tourist information centers, and places of interest.

    Paragraph 3: Express appreciation for their help and ask specifically that the information be sent as quickly as possible so that plans can be formulated.

50-2

(Use the rough draft from Problem 50-1.)

50-3

New Hampshire Chamber of Commerce / 15 Oak Drive
South / Concord. NH 03824–4210

SKILL IMPROVEMENT

(Refer to the Skill Improvement exercise in LESSON 30.)

DIRECTIONS: Type the accuracy and speed lines 3 times each. Take a 1-minute timing on each line, repeating copy as necessary. Then take a 1-minute timing on the control paragraph with 28 wpm as your goal. Indent the first line 5 spaces.

MARGINS: 50-space line
SINGLE SPACING

SKILL IMPROVEMENT

Accuracy:

Sue may stop here on the day you buy the new car.   10

Speed:

You will surely be proud of how well you can run.   10

Control Paragraph:

    A group of boys stood near the small fire and   10
hoped they would get warm. It was a very cold day   20
when the five of them fell into the icy stream. A   30
scream from one of them led a passing hunter close   40
to the site of their mishap. If it were not for a   50
person who was alert, they may well have perished.   60

| 1 | 2 | 3 | 4 | 5 | 6 | 7 | 8 | 9 | 10 |

DIRECTIONS: Using the envelope size indicated, or paper cut to size, type the following addresses in good form, placing special notations in the appropriate locations. Use your name and return address. Erase and correct all errors.

49-5

ENVELOPE SIZE	ADDRESS	SPECIAL NOTATION
Small	Mr. Jack Roberts The Hayden Hotel 5 Loop Center Chicago, IL 60690-6431	CERTIFIED HOLD FOR ARRIVAL
Small	Mrs. Marjorie Marshall 894 Seaview Street (Apt. 3) Long Beach, CA 90402-8101	PLEASE FORWARD
Large	Ms. Kathy Demford The Large Company 34 Market Street San Francisco, CA 94113-4869	PERSONAL SPECIAL DELIVERY
Large	Mr. Henry Arthur The McMillan Company 207 Moore Avenue Portland, OR 92843-2070	REGISTERED

DIRECTIONS: Take a 1-minute timing on the control paragraph, repeating copy as necessary. Remember, your goal is to type it at 43 wpm with no more than 1 error per minute.

MARGINS: 70-space line
SINGLE SPACE

SKILL IMPROVEMENT

(Refer to the Skill Improvement exercise in LESSON 29.)

LESSON 29

OBJECTIVE: To learn how to spread letters on the writing line when it is necessary.

DIRECTIONS: Type the warm-up line 3 times with <u>control</u> as your goal.

MARGINS: 50-space line

DIRECTIONS: Type each of the following sentences WITH THE ERROR. Following the directions on each line, erase and spread the correction as indicated.

MARGINS: 55-space line
DOUBLE SPACING

REMEMBER: If you are spreading letters, you will need to move a little bit more than a full space for each letter.

DIRECTIONS: Type the accuracy and speed lines 3 times each. Take a 1-minute timing on each line, repeating copy as necessary. Then take a 1-minute timing on the control paragraph with 29 wpm as your goal. Indent the first line 5 spaces.

MARGINS: 50-space line
SINGLE SPACING

SPREADING TECHNIQUES

GOAL: To type 29 or more wpm with no more than 1 error per minute.

STRETCH FOR SPEED.

WARM-UP

More folks eat dinner out on Friday than on Monday.

On a piece of paper type the following sentence as shown:

    Send the order to-day collect.

It is necessary to remove the hyphen in the word "today." To do that, the 5 letters must be spread into the 6 spaces to avoid erasing the rest of the line.

To spread a correction—to make it fill an extra space—you must spread out the word a half space to the *right*, using one of the methods of carriage control shown in LESSON 28, depending on your typewriter. Now, following the procedure outlined in LESSON 28, erase and correct the word "today."

29-1

		Change	To
1. The price is too unreasonable.		price	cost
2. His secretary is allways on time.		allways	always
3. I found the story interesting.		found	find
4. The required problem onely takes five minutes.		onely	only
5. She could report to us next week.		could	will

SKILL IMPROVEMENT

Accuracy:
Bill was sad when he was required to leave school. 10

Speed:
I must call you soon so that you will not miss me. 10

Control Paragraph:

```
     The road that runs past our house is the same   10
as the one which goes down to the lake.  They tell  20
me that the fish in the lake are very quick to eat  30
any bait you might use on the hook.  You will have  40
to be very skillful and quiet when you try to bait  50
the hook.  I wish you luck with the catch.          58
```

| 1 | 2 | 3 | 4 | 5 | 6 | 7 | 8 | 9 | 10 |

DIRECTIONS: Type two No. 10 envelopes, using the following addresses. Erase and correct all errors. Include your name and return address. Remember to even out the lines and aim for correct placement.

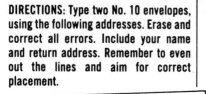

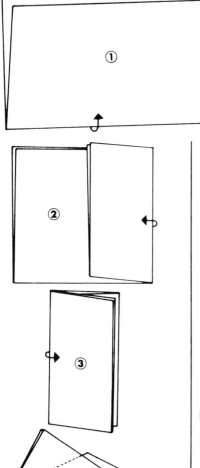

COMMERCIAL ENVELOPE (NO. 6¾)

DIRECTIONS: Using a small (No. 6¾) envelope, type the following name and address from Problem 48-1. Mark the envelope SPECIAL DELIVERY. Include your name and return address. Fold the letter typed in Problem 48-1 and insert it into the envelope.

DIRECTIONS: Using a large (No. 10) envelope, type the name and address from Problem 48-2. Mark the envelope CERTIFIED. Include your name and return address. Fold the letter typed in Problem 48-2 and insert it into the envelope.

49-2

Send the first envelope to:
Johnson Manufacturing Company
24 Olson Street
Lansing, MI 48823-1244

Send the second envelope to:
Mrs. Joanne Torrero
Faculty Director
Success Business School
675 East 25 Street
New York, NY 10016-6750

Procedure for Folding and Inserting Letters

To fold letters for the appropriate-size envelopes, follow the instructions below. Note the illustrations.

◆ FOLDING FOR THE SMALL ENVELOPE

Step 1: Fold up the bottom edge to about ¼″ from the top edge.

Step 2: Fold across from right to left a little less than ⅓ of the way.

Step 3: Fold again left to right allowing ¼″ thumb space.

Step 4: Hold letter up with thumb portion toward you. Insert into envelope.

FOLDING FOR THE LARGE ENVELOPE ◆

Step 1: Fold up from the bottom a little less than ⅓ of the way.

Step 2: Fold top third down, allowing ¼″ thumb space.

Step 3: Hold letter toward you with thumb portion up. Insert into envelope.

LEGAL ENVELOPE (NO. 10)

For practice, using the letters you typed in Problems 44-1, 45-1, 46-1, and 46-2, fold and insert them into the appropriate envelopes from Problems 49-1 and 49-2.

49-3

Mason Information Services / Elm Building /
55 Orange Boulevard / Miami, FL 33442-1654

49-4

Mr. Bertram N. Holmes, Director / High School
Travel Program / 1802 East Mifflin Street /
Chicago, IL 60690-3192

LESSON 30

OBJECTIVE: To review correcting techniques, crowding and spreading, typing from rough draft with proofreaders' symbols, and following the warning bell with even margins and lines.

DIRECTIONS: Type the warm-up line 3 times with _speed_ as your goal.

MARGINS: 50-space line

DIRECTIONS: Type the following edited paragraphs, using a 5-space paragraph indention and beginning on line 13. Follow the bell as you type. Even out lines and margins, and if you must divide words, be sure to follow the correct word division rules. Proofread carefully, and correct your errors neatly and accurately.

MARGINS: 60-space line
DOUBLE SPACING

REVIEW OF CORRECTING TECHNIQUES

GOAL: To type 30 or more wpm with no more than 1 error per minute.

NEVER DIVIDE A ONE-SYLLABLE WORD.

WARM-UP

Sally mailed six letters before she left for work.

30-1

5 Even though you are learning to type for personal reasons, have you ever considered using the skill you are learning to gain employment? There is quite a strong demand for good typists, for people (can who) type rapidly and accurately enough to aid those in buiness with the flow of their paperwork and correspondence. ¶Learning to type will also give you the primary skill necessary to operate new word processing equipment, telegraph and telex machines, and teletypewriters. Satistical typists (those people who prepare charts involving many figures) are sought after and paid well for their specialized abiliy to use the typewriter.

You can use your typing in many ways. Look through a newspaper and check the want ads under "Typists" to see just what the demand is in your area. You are sure to find many opportunities. ¶Remember that if you develop your the touch technique to the best of your ability, can improve your speed with each passing day, and can concentrate on typing accuratel, your "personal" skill can be used in many employable wys. Never forget that you can earn and type at the same time. There are summer jobs and part-time jobs waiting rady for the qualified. Both men as well as and women are needed to fill the ever-increasing demand.

- All addresses are single-spaced and blocked.
- Use state abbreviations prescribed by the Postal Service. (See chart that follows.)
- Zip codes are typed 2 spaces after state abbreviation. Note the use of longer zip codes.
- Return address begins:
    3 lines down from top edge
    3 spaces in from left edge
- Write out words such as *Street, Avenue, Boulevard.*
- Directions (North, South, East, West) may or may not be abbreviated. Your consideration should be to EVEN OUT THE LINE.
- Apartment numbers or building room numbers must follow and be on the same line as the street address.
- The ATTENTION or the c/o ("Care of") line must be placed on the second line of the main address. Do not type anything *below* the main address.
- The inside address on the letter should conform to the envelope. In both places it should be typed exactly the same.
- Post Office Notations:
    SPECIAL DELIVERY
    AIRMAIL
    CERTIFIED
    REGISTERED
  Type in caps on line 8, ending about 3 spaces before right edge.
- Personal Notations:
    PERSONAL
    CONFIDENTIAL
    PLEASE FORWARD
    HOLD FOR ARRIVAL
  Type in caps on line 8 or double-spaced below return address. Begin 3 spaces from left edge.

POSTAL SERVICE STATE ABBREVIATIONS

Alabama	AL	Kansas	KS	North Dakota	ND
Alaska	AK	Kentucky	KY	Ohio	OH
Arizona	AZ	Louisiana	LA	Oklahoma	OK
Arkansas	AR	Maine	ME	Oregon	OR
California	CA	Maryland	MD	Pennsylvania	PA
Colorado	CO	Massachusetts	MA	Puerto Rico	PR
Connecticut	CT	Michigan	MI	Rhode Island	RI
Delaware	DE	Minnesota	MN	South Carolina	SC
District of	DC	Mississippi	MS	South Dakota	SD
Columbia		Missouri	MO	Tennessee	TN
Florida	FL	Montana	MT	Texas	TX
Georgia	GA	Nebraska	NE	Utah	UT
Guam	GU	Nevada	NV	Virginia	VA
Hawaii	HI	New Hampshire	NH	Vermont	VT
Idaho	ID	New Jersey	NJ	Washington	WA
Illinois	IL	New Mexico	NM	Wisconsin	WI
Indiana	IN	New York	NY	West Virginia	WV
Iowa	IA	North Carolina	NC	Wyoming	WY

For local zip codes, consult your local telephone directory. For distant zip codes, consult the Post Office for the official Zip Code Directory.

DIRECTIONS: Type two No. 6¾ envelopes, using the following addresses. Include your name and return address.

49-1

Send the first envelope to:
Computer Equipment Corporation
1900 Fifth Avenue
New York, NY 10021-1900

Send the second envelope to:
The Boulder Valley Hotel
22 Mountain Boulevard
Boulder, CO 92014-4685

DIRECTIONS: Type the accuracy and speed lines 3 times each. Take a 1-minute timing on each line, repeating copy as necessary. Then take a 1-minute timing on the control paragraph with 30 wpm as your goal. Indent the first line 5 spaces.

MARGINS: 50-space line
SINGLE SPACING

SKILL IMPROVEMENT

Accuracy:

The group left here when your talk was made today. 10

Speed:

The cattle were jammed in a small pen on the hill. 10

Control Paragraph:

In the world most oceans are very large. One 10
of them is also very deep in several spots. Ships 20
which sail on the oceans of the world may run into 30
many severe storms. Oceans serve as a source of a 40
great deal of pleasure for some, as food for other 50
people, and yet man does not know much about them. 60

| 1 | 2 | 3 | 4 | 5 | 6 | 7 | 8 | 9 | 10 |

LESSON 49

TYPING ENVELOPES

GOAL: To type 43 or more wpm with no more than 1 error per minute.

FASTER, FASTER- YOU CAN DO IT!

OBJECTIVE: To learn how to type various kinds of envelopes.

DIRECTIONS: Type the warm-up line 3 times with <u>accuracy</u> as your goal.

MARGINS: 70-space line

WARM-UP

The best way to improve your typewriting skill is
to have daily practice.

The envelope is as important as the letter. It is the first impression of you that your correspondent gets. Therefore, it is IMPERATIVE that you type the envelope ACCURATELY, NEATLY, AND IN GOOD FORM.

Use the following information as a guide to typing envelopes. The rules given conform with the U.S. Postal Service equipment, the Optical Character Reader (OCR). The envelopes illustrated are those most commonly used for personal business letters. The No. 6¾ commercial or standard small envelope measures 6½ × 3⅝ inches; the No. 10 legal or standard large envelope measures 9½ × 4⅛ inches.

Procedure for Typing Envelopes

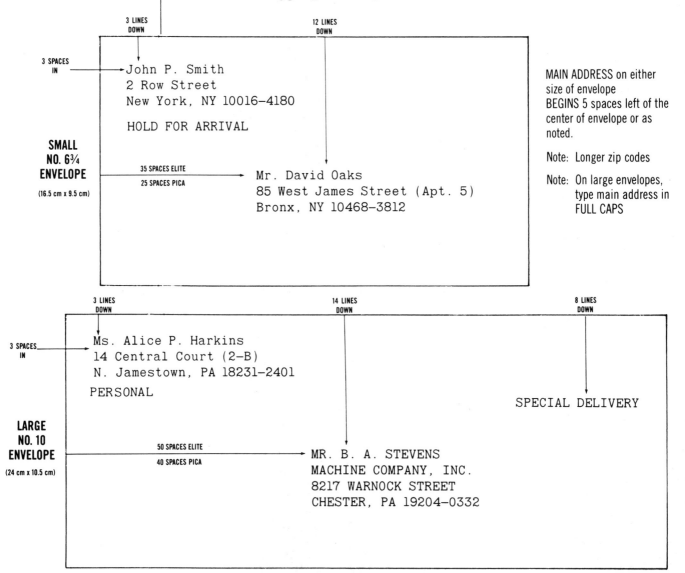

MAIN ADDRESS on either size of envelope
BEGINS 5 spaces left of the center of envelope or as noted.

Note: Longer zip codes

Note: On large envelopes, type main address in FULL CAPS

CHAPTER

IV

CENTERING

48-2

DIRECTIONS: Follow the directions in Problem 48-1 except use semi-blocked style with open punctuation. Paragraph this letter yourself. Keep in mind that most letters should include about 3 paragraphs: the introductory paragraph, the main message, and the closing. A paragraph includes sentences surrounding one central idea. SAVE THIS LETTER.

Mr. Bertram N. Holmes, Director / High School
Travel Program / 1802 East Mifflin Street /
Chicago, IL 60690 /

Mr. Holmes
Dear ~~Sir~~

I have read with interest your brochure for high school students who wish to travel in organized groups during the summer. It seems like a great idea for a person of my age to have such an experience. I am particularly eager to ~~see~~ have the details on the "Major Cities of Europe," your Group Trip No. 4, which leaves on June 28 and returns on August 27. My parents are willing to pay for this trip. Am I correct that the cost is $1,000? If so, could you please send me all the necessary information and forms to fill in. The prospect of such a trip is very exciting. I look forward to hearing from you soon.

Yours very truly

DIRECTIONS: Take a 1-minute timing on the control paragraph, repeating copy as necessary. Remember, your goal is to type it at 42 wpm with no more than 1 error per minute.

MARGINS: 70-space line
SINGLE SPACING

SKILL IMPROVEMENT

(Refer to the Skill Improvement exercise in LESSON 28.)

LESSON 31

OBJECTIVE: To learn to center horizontally by using the backspace key.

DIRECTIONS: Type the warm-up line 3 times with <u>accuracy</u> as your goal.

MARGINS: 60-space line

REMEMBER: The center point is 42 on pica typewriters, 51 on elite machines.

DIRECTIONS: Using the backspace method just described, center these lines and then check your work to see that it is centered properly. Use double spacing.

DIRECTIONS: On a half sheet of paper, center each of these names. Type the first line on line 13 from the top edge of the paper. Use double spacing.

HORIZONTAL CENTERING

GOAL: To type 31 or more wpm with no more than 1 error per minute.

WARM-UP

Typing accurately is more important than typing rapidly.

Horizontal centering is the arrangement of words, titles, and the like so that they are centered evenly ACROSS the page. Correct horizontal centering means that there are the same number of blank spaces on each side of the word or line of type. On most electronic typewriters, horizontal centering can be done automatically by using special function keys. Check your machine to see how this is done.

Procedure for Centering Horizontally Using the Backspace Method

- Make sure the paper guide is set at 0.
- Clear the margins and tabs. (Set the margins at the extreme left and extreme right of the carriage.)
- Move to the center of the paper and backspace once for every 2 letters or spaces.

For example, to center the words TYPING IS FUN:

- Backspace once for every 2 letters or spaces.
- Ignore the last letter.
- Consider the space between words as a letter.

        Backspace once for TY
        Backspace again for PI
        Backspace again for NG
        Backspace again for space I
        Backspace again for S space
        Backspace again for FU (ignore the N)

- Now type the words and check to see if the line is centered. Remove the paper from the typewriter, fold it in half vertically, and, holding it up to the light, see if the beginning and ending of the line meet. It is acceptable to be 2 or 3 spaces off.

31-1

TYPEWRITING

WALLINGTON HIGH SCHOOL

CHOCOLATE FUDGE COOKIES

ANGHOUSE PUBLICATIONS

31-2

SAM ROLAND
JOHN ORLON
PHIL COLBERT
STAN SOMMERS
HARRY MORRISON

Note that if you have done the problem correctly, the letter "O" should be aligned.

LESSON 48

OBJECTIVE: To learn to type handwritten personal business letters with copy.

DIRECTIONS: Type the warm-up line 3 times with <u>speed</u> as your goal.

MARGINS: 70-space line

DIRECTIONS: Type the following unarranged handwritten personal business letter in good form, following the bell and dividing words properly only when necessary. Use blocked style and mixed punctuation. Prepare 1 copy, using your street address, city, state, zip code, and today's date in the heading, and use your own name in the closing. Don't forget to sign your name. SAVE THIS LETTER.

MARGINS: 60-space line
SINGLE SPACING

TYPING HANDWRITTEN PERSONAL BUSINESS LETTERS WITH COPY

KEEP YOUR EYES ON THE COPY.

GOAL: To type 42 or more wpm with no more than 1 error per minute.

WARM-UP

The dazzling, sizzling, and simmering sun suggests the ocean is close.

48-1

Mason Information Services / Elm Building / 55 Orange Boulevard / Miami, FL 33442 /

Gentlemen:

I am interested in studying abroad in my junior year in college. I have heard that you have prepared lists of schools, their locations, and the kinds of foreign programs that are offered.

Could you please send me whatever information ~~that~~ you can so that I might make appropriate plans. If the information ~~that~~ you mail contains the cost of such programs, that would also be very helpful.

~~Thank you for your help that~~ Any aid you can give me, will be appreciated! I know that if I begin my search early enough, perhaps I'll have ~~just~~ ~~that much~~ more chance of finding a program that meets my needs.

Yours truly,

DIRECTIONS: On a half sheet of paper, center each of these names. Begin typing on line 13. Use double spacing.

MARIANNE LESTER
ANNE GOLDEN
PATSY CLARK
LEAH WILCOX
MARCY SALMON
JO—ALICE LORRIE

If you have done the problem correctly, the letter "L" should be aligned. In typing the last name in the list, did you remember to release the shift lock to type the hyphen?

SKILL IMPROVEMENT

DIRECTIONS: Type the accuracy and speed lines 3 times each. Take a 1-minute timing on each line, repeating copy as necessary. Then take a 1-minute timing on the control paragraph with 31 wpm as your goal. Indent the first line 5 spaces.

MARGINS: 60-space line
SINGLE SPACING

Accuracy:

We should be thankful for the	6
lovely trees and protect them.	12

Speed:

We used to have to write only	6
a letter every day to qualify.	12

Control Paragraph:

The larger any company is, the more problems will occur	12
in relation to human relations skills. It is a fact that in	24
large businesses more people lose their jobs because they do	36
not know how to get along with others than because of a lack	48
of technical skills. This statement does not in any way im—	60
ply that good skills are not important. What it really says	72
is that one must possess so much more. Our school can serve	84
a real need in this area because we offer classes which will	96
assist you in developing these skills.	104

| 1 | 2 | 3 | 4 | 5 | 6 | 7 | 8 | 9 | 10 | 11 | 12 |

DIRECTIONS: Insert into the typewriter an original, a piece of carbon paper, and a piece of copy paper. Set a 5-space tab indention. Following the warning bell, type this handwritten paragraph. Erase and neatly correct all errors on the original and copy. Keep in mind good correcting techniques.

**MARGINS: 60-space line
DOUBLE SPACING**

REMEMBER: Proofread carefully BE-FORE REMOVING PAPER FROM THE TYPEWRITER so that errors can be easily corrected.

DIRECTIONS: Take a 1-minute timing on the control paragraph, repeating copy as necessary. Remember, your goal is to type it at 42 wpm with no more than 1 error per minute.

**MARGINS: 70-space line
SINGLE SPACING**

47-2

Make your ~~carbon~~ copy as important as your original. Take the time, erase and correct carefully and accurately. Take pride in your work. After all, it is an example of you—it is almost like a first impression. You would agree, I am sure, that first impressions are important!

SKILL IMPROVEMENT

(Refer to the Skill Improvement exercise in LESSON 27.)

LESSON

32

HORIZONTAL SPREAD CENTERING

TYPE BY TOUCH ONLY.

GOAL: To type 32 or more wpm with no more than 1 error per minute.

OBJECTIVE: To learn the spread centering method.

DIRECTIONS: Type the warm-up line 3 times with <u>control</u> as your goal.

MARGINS: 60-space line

WARM-UP

A good business attitude is important to future success.

Horizontal spread centering is sometimes used to display a line more prominently than centering it in the usual manner. In horizontal spread centering, a space is inserted after EACH letter and 3 spaces BETWEEN words. Notice how the "spread" heading looks compared to the one centered in the conventional way:

```
        WORD DIVISION
  W O R D   D I V I S I O N
```

To center a spread heading, use the standard backspacing method. For practice, spread center the following example as you read the directions.

EXAMPLE:
Spread center the title WORD DIVISION by "tabbing" to the center point of the typewriter. Backspace once for *each* letter in the line *except the last letter* and backspace once for each blank area left between words. Now type WORD DIVISION, leaving a space between letters and 3 spaces between words.

DIRECTIONS: On a half sheet of paper, spread center the following lines. Begin on line 14 and use double spacing.

32-1

```
        A T T E N T I O N
          S P E C I A L
     D I N N E R   M E N U
          T H E   E N D
```

If you have done the problem correctly, the letter "E" will be aligned.

DIRECTIONS: On a half sheet of paper, center the following lines. Begin on line 11 and use double spacing.

32-2

```
        A N N O U N C E M E N T
                ----
         There will be a meeting of
            THE RALLY CLUB
          in the Gym on Friday
        FROM THREE TO FOUR-THIRTY

                ----
```

LESSON 47

OBJECTIVE: To learn the proper use of carbons.

DIRECTIONS: Type the warm-up line 3 times with <u>control</u> as your goal.

MARGINS: 70-space line

USING CARBONS

GOAL: To type 42 or more wpm with no more than 1 error per minute.

ERASE CLEANLY, BUT DON'T SCRUB.

WARM-UP

How to develop human potential is always a very
stimulating subject.

Make it a HABIT to prepare a copy (either carbon or photostat) of all correspondence. It is an important and convenient reference of the date of the correspondence, the person or firm to whom you wrote, and the purpose of such writing.

Inserting Carbon Paper

1, Insert carbon paper between the original and-copy. THE SHINY SIDE OF THE CARBON SHOULD BE FACING YOU as it is rolled into the typewriter.
2. Many people use onionskin paper for copies. Carbon packs are also available and include a carbon and onionskin paper attached. These are simply placed behind the original and rolled into the typewriter. The copy paper should be towards you as it is rolled into the machine.

Using Carbon Paper

Most commercial carbon paper can be used several times. However, avoid using worn or wrinkled carbons, which will produce "trees" on your copies, making them difficult to read.

Procedure for Correcting Copies with Carbon

1. An ERASING SHIELD is used in the correction of carbons. It is placed between the original and carbon when erasing the original. This prevents smudges on the copy. .
2. An easy substitute for an erasing shield is a folded 3 × 5 card. It is harder than regular paper, yet flexible enough to curve around the typewriter roller.
3. Erase carbons first, then the original. The erasing shield must be moved forward or backward as you erase. Use a regular typing eraser for the original but a softer pencil eraser on the copy.
4. Erase in a slow, circular motion, brushing crumbs to the sides of the typewriter. Remember to avoid "scrubbing."

DIRECTIONS: Insert into the typewriter an original, a piece of carbon paper, and a piece of copy paper. Type the following sentences, correcting each one according to the directions given. Use crowding and spreading if necessary (see LESSONS 28 and 29). Erase and neatly correct the original and the copy. Keep in mind good correcting techniques.

MARGINS: 60-space line
DOUBLE SPACING

47-1

		Change	To
1.	The magazine is on sail.	sail	sale
2.	Remember to eras neatly.	eras	erase
3.	Use the eraser shielld appropriately.	shielld	shield
4.	Use and calculate odd and even figures.	figures	numbers
5.	Jerry and Anne-Marie Martin were late.	Jerry	Gerald

DIRECTIONS: On a half sheet of paper, center the following lines. Begin on line 13 and use double spacing.

THE SEWING CLUB
announces its
ANNUAL QUILT EXHIBIT
Sunday, June 18
ON THE CHURCH GROUNDS

DIRECTIONS: Type the accuracy and speed lines 3 times each. Take a 1-minute timing on each line, repeating copy as necessary. Then take a 1-minute timing on the control paragraph with 32 wpm as your goal. Indent the first line 5 spaces.

MARGINS: 60-space line
SINGLE SPACING

SKILL IMPROVEMENT

Accuracy:

The girls did not see the six	6
big men who hid the car today.	12

Speed:

Mark told her Mary wanted them	6
both to work very hard today.	12

Control Paragraph:

Frequently the best workers find that they get tired of	12
the chores they must do day in and day out. When people are	24
tired or bored is just the time they must dig in and try all	36
the more to do their level best. Many times even the one in	48
a higher position finds that he or she will get bored. When	60
the days begin to drag, it is time to take a vacation. Once	72
the workers are away from their desks, their attitude should	84
improve. Then they will be glad to return to their offices.	96

  | 1 | 2 | 3 | 4 | 5 | 6 | 7 | 8 | 9 | 10 | 11 | 12 |

DIRECTIONS: Follow the directions for Problem 46-1 except use semi-blocked style with mixed punctuation. SAVE THIS LETTER.

46-2

Mrs. Joanne Torrero / Faculty Director / Success Business School / 675 East 25 Street / New York, NY 10016 / Dear Mrs. Torrero: /

Thank you for interviewing me this morning. I appreciate the time you took to explain thoroughly the opportunities available with your school.

Although I am not looking for another full-time position at the present time, I would be available for a summer position or as a substitute in your evening division.

I enjoyed meeting you and having the chance to converse. Best wishes for continued success with your school.

Very truly yours, / Your name

DIRECTIONS: Take a 1-minute timing on the control paragraph, repeating copy as necessary. Remember, your goal is to type it at 42 wpm with no more than 1 error per minute.

MARGINS: 70-space line
SINGLE SPACING

SKILL IMPROVEMENT

(Refer to the Skill Improvement exercise in LESSON 26.)

LESSON 33

OBJECTIVE: To learn to center vertically by using the HUSH method.

DIRECTIONS: Type the warm-up line 3 times with <u>speed</u> as your goal.

MARGINS: 60-space line

VERTICAL CENTERING

GOAL: To type 33 or more wpm with no more than 1 error per minute.

USE THE HUSH METHOD!

WARM-UP

A job interview requires you to dress in a proper
way.

Correct vertical placement means that there are the same number of blank lines at the top and bottom of the page. *One* vertical inch equals 6 typing lines. If your paper is 11 inches long, there are 66 vertical lines (11 inches × 6 lines per inch) on the paper.

Procedure for Centering Vertically Using the HUSH Method

H = HAVE   Number of lines you <u>have</u> to work with:
     Full sheet = 66 lines
     Half sheet = 33 lines

U = USE   Number of lines the problem will <u>use</u>. Count all lines, including blank lines, in the problem.

S = SUBTRACT   <u>Subtract</u> the number of lines used from the number of lines available.

H = HALF   Divide the answer in <u>half</u>. This tells how many <u>blank</u> lines to leave at the top; start typing on the next line. If you end up with a fraction, drop it.

Here are two examples:

H =	66	(full sheet)	H =	33	(half sheet)
U =	<u>24</u>	(lines in problem)	U =	<u>24</u>	(lines in problem)
S =	42		S =	9	
H =	21	(blank lines on top)	H =	4½	(drop the ½)
Start on line 22.			Start on line 5.		

Note the following:

1. When you *triple*-space, you leave *2 blank lines* and type on the *third* line:

     Typed Word
     Blank Line
     Blank Line
     Typed Word

REMEMBER that the number of blank lines is always 1 less than the number of times you return the carriage. To double-space (leave 1 blank line), return the carriage 2 times. To triple-space (leave 2 blank lines), return the carriage 3 times.

2. When you *double*-space, you leave 1 *blank line* and type on the *second* line:

     Typed Word
     Blank Line
     Typed Word

3. When you *single*-space, you leave *no blank lines* and type on the *next* line:

     Typed Word
     Typed Word

DIRECTIONS: Count the number of lines you use to center the following vertically, using a full sheet of paper, with a triple space after the title and a double space between the items. Then type the copy.

33-1

     <u>REASONS FOR JOINING THE CLUB</u>

       THE DOUBLECARD

       CASH ADVANTAGE

       TRAVEL INSURANCE

       EMERGENCY CASH

LESSON 46

TYPE AREA CODES IN PARENTHESES.

TYPING UNARRANGED PERSONAL BUSINESS LETTERS

GOAL: To type 42 or more wpm with no more than 1 error per minute.

OBJECTIVE: To type personal business letters from unarranged copy.

DIRECTIONS: Type the warm-up line 3 times with <u>accuracy</u> as your goal.

MARGINS: 70-space line

WARM-UP

The special office was moved to the side of the home for all to visit.

NOTE: Diagonals (/) are used to indicate the separation of individual lines of addresses and closings in letters. These are *not* to be typed when doing the problems.

DIRECTIONS: Type the following unarranged personal business letter in good form, following the warning bell and dividing words properly only when necessary. Use blocked style and open punctuation. Use your street address, city, state, zip code, and today's date in the heading and your own name in the closing. Don't forget to sign your name. Correct errors as you type. SAVE THIS LETTER.

MARGINS: 60-space line
SINGLE SPACING

46-1

Johnson Manufacturing Corp. / 24 Olson Street / Lansing, MI 48823 /

Gentlemen

Enclosed is my resume, which gives full particulars concerning my qualifications and experience.

I feel that I can adequately handle the position described in the ad of last Sunday. My desire to learn and grow in the job is strong, and I am sure you would be pleased with my capabilities.

May I have an interview? I would be more than pleased to meet with you at a date and time that is mutually convenient. Please call me at (517) 351-0477.

Yours truly / Your name

DIRECTIONS: On a full sheet of paper, center this problem vertically and type each of the lines horizontally centered. Use double spacing.

33-2

S P E C I A L   R E P O R T

on

COMPETITIVE AIR FARES

between

N E W   Y O R K   A N D   C A L I F O R N I A

Prepared for

Dr. Nelson L. Angus

by

G. Marion Frick

DIRECTIONS: On a half sheet of paper, center this announcement vertically and horizontally. Use single spacing.

33-3

THE NEXT REHEARSAL OF
THE GARRET MOUNTAIN ORCHESTRA
WILL BE HELD
THURSDAY, APRIL 30, AT 7 p.m.
PLEASE BE PROMPT!

DIRECTIONS: On a half sheet of paper, center this menu vertically and horizontally. Use triple spacing after the title and double spacing between the other lines.

33-4

WEDNESDAY LUNCHEON SPECIAL
MINESTRONE SOUP
GRILLED CHEESE WITH TOMATO AND BACON
INDIVIDUAL SALAD
RASPBERRY SHERBERT
COFFEE, TEA, OR MILK

DIRECTIONS: Type the accuracy and speed lines 3 times each. Take a 1-minute timing on each line, repeating copy as necessary. Then take a 1-minute timing on the control paragraph with 33 wpm as your goal. Indent the first line 5 spaces.

MARGINS: 60-space line
SINGLE SPACING

SKILL IMPROVEMENT

Accuracy:

Mary said she would return your	6
gray suit early in the week.	12

Speed:

The entire team received many	6
honors for their perfect work.	12

Control Paragraph:

Many of us fall into the habit of thinking that we will	12
be able to get a new lease on life when the thought comes to	24
our mind. Frequently we merely coast along thinking that if	36
a big break comes our way we will then sit up and take note.	48
If you are in the habit of coasting, you will turn out to be	60
a loser and not move forward.	66

| 1 | 2 | 3 | 4 | 5 | 6 | 7 | 8 | 9 | 10 | 11 | 12 |

Lesson 33: VERTICAL CENTERING **53**

DIRECTIONS: Following the directions for 45-1, make a copy of this personal business letter. Note that it is typed in *blocked* style with open punctuation (no punctuation after salutation or closing).

```
                          Your street address
                          Your city, state, zip code
                          Today's date


          Registrar's Office
          Hilton College of Sciences
          8246 Lower Boulevard
          Phoenix, AZ 85022

          Gentlemen

          I am a high school junior and will be graduating
          at the end of the next school year.  Your college
          is known to have a fine reputation and an excel-
          lent program in the sciences.  Since I am eager to
          pursue a premed course, I would like to apply
          early.

          Would you please send me the information I need
          for making application, such as a catalog, appli-
          cation form, and other pertinent forms necessary
          for completing the process.  I would also appreci-
          ate any additional information about your college
          and the courses it offers which you think will be
          helpful to me.

          Your cooperation will be most appreciated.

                          Yours very truly


                          Your name
```

DIRECTIONS: Take a 1-minute timing on the control paragraph, repeating copy as necessary. Remember, your goal is to type it at 41 wpm with no more than 1 error per minute.

MARGINS: 70-space line
SINGLE SPACING

SKILL IMPROVEMENT

(Refer to the Skill Improvement exercise in LESSON 25.)

LESSON 34

CENTERING AN EXACT COPY

GOAL: To type 34 or more wpm with no more than 1 error per minute.

SPREAD CENTERING IS EFFECTIVE.

OBJECTIVE: To practice typing an exact copy, including vertical and horizontal centering.

DIRECTIONS: Type the warm-up line 3 times with <u>accuracy</u> as your goal.

MARGINS: 60-space line

WARM-UP

A good typist is one who has the ability to think ahead.

Procedure for Typing an Exact Copy

- Clear all margins and tab stops.
- Determine the vertical starting point.
- On the vertical starting line, backspace center and type any titles or headings.
- Backspace center the KEY LINE of the copy. This may be the longest line or a series of lines that make up the longest line. Remember that the key line covers all the spaces that will be used from the farthest left to the farthest right.
- Set your left margin at the point where you complete the centering of the key line. Do not set a right margin.
- Type the copy line for line as you see it. Remember to return the carriage the same number of times at the end of each line as you see in the problem.
- To check centering:

Checking Vertical Centering: Fold the paper top to bottom without creasing and hold it up to the light. The first and last lines of the problem should be no more than 4 lines off.

Checking Horizontal Centering: Fold the paper in half left to right without creasing and hold it up to the light. The first and last letters of the key line should be no more than 2 or 3 spaces off.

DIRECTIONS: Make an exact copy of this problem. Center it both vertically and horizontally. Correct all typing errors before removing the paper from the typewriter. Check to see that you have centered correctly (see above).

34-1

LEARN A LANGUAGE

T O D A Y !

      Come to our school! Observe our in-
struction. See for yourself how easily and
quickly you will be able to speak, understand, read, and write the language of your
choice. We have qualified instructors and
the newest, modern methods.

Free Lessons Every Monday

Don't Wait--Call Today. Phone 555-3001 Now!

LESSON 45

TYPING ARRANGED PERSONAL BUSINESS LETTERS

GOAL: To type 41 or more wpm with no more than 1 error per minute.

OBJECTIVE: To learn to type an arranged personal business letter.

DIRECTIONS: Type the warm-up line 3 times with <u>speed</u> as your goal.

MARGINS: 70-space line

DIRECTIONS: Make a copy of the following personal business letter. Note that it is typed in *semi-blocked* style with mixed punctuation (a colon after the salutation and a comma after the complimentary close). Use your street address, city, state, and zip code in the heading, and your own name in the closing. Don't forget to include your signature. Proofread the letter carefully and circle errors. SAVE THE LETTER.

MARGINS: 60-space line
SINGLE SPACING

WARM-UP

There was a time when life was easy and little
attention paid to work.

NOTE: Men do NOT type or sign the word "Mr." in the closing, but women may use "Miss," "Ms.," or "Mrs." in the typed signature.

45-1

```
                              Your street address
                              Your city, state, zip
                              Today's date


The Boulder Valley Hotel
22 Mountain Boulevard
Boulder, CO 92104

Gentlemen:

     My family and I will be traveling through
Colorado for our spring vacation.  We would like
to spend some time in Boulder and will be staying
there on Sunday, April 15, and Monday, April 16.

     We would like to make reservation for two
medium-priced rooms with private baths and twin
beds for those two days.  Is there space available?
Is a deposit required?

     We would appreciate hearing from you as soon
as possible so that we can finalize our plans.
Thank you for your cooperation.

                         Very truly yours,


                         Your name
```

DIRECTIONS: Follow the directions for 34-1.

34-2

F R E E   L E C T U R E   S E R I E S

on

CHINA TODAY

We are happy to announce a series of lectures to be given by a notable Chinese historian during the week of April 1. The topics to be covered will include such areas of interest as:

Influence from Past Chinese Culture
Living in China Today
Today's Language of the Chinese
Education in China Today

The lectures will take place at the University Center each day at 4:00 p.m. Since space is limited to 100 persons, we advise you to sign up now. In the past these lectures have proved to be quite a success, and we know that you won't want to miss a single one.

QUESTION—ANSWER PERIOD WILL FOLLOW EACH LECTURE.

DIRECTIONS: Make an exact typed copy of this HANDWRITTEN problem. Center it both vertically and horizontally. Correct all errors. Check to see that you have centered correctly.

34-3

HAPPY EATING!

After you have had a hectic day, don't you wish you could sit down and really have a snack that would be appetizing, nutritious, and also relaxing?

Sure you do!

DIRECTIONS: Type the accuracy and speed lines 3 times each. Take a 1-minute timing on each line, repeating copy as necessary. Then take a 1-minute timing on the control paragraph with 34 wpm as your goal. Indent the first line 5 spaces.

MARGINS: 60-space line
SINGLE SPACING

SKILL IMPROVEMENT

Accuracy:

The sale of soft drinks should	6
bring extra cash for charity.	12

Speed:

We can serve you if you will	6
just tell us how we can assist.	12

Control Paragraph:

Most of us have some ambition because many of us desire	12
the good things that are not within our reach at the moment.	24
The only way to get the things we want is to keep trying and	36
we will succeed. Many times we will run into problems as we	48
strive for the things we want in life. Without problems, we	60
would have rather dull lives. Whenever you are upset at the	72
problems with which you are faced, think of these words.	83

| 1 | 2 | 3 | 4 | 5 | 6 | 7 | 8 | 9 | 10 | 11 | 12 |

Letters That Require Two or More Pages

There may be times when you have to type a 2-page letter. In this case:

1. Type to within 1 inch from the bottom of the first page.
2. Try to be in the middle of a paragraph when you go from the first page to the second.
3. There must be at least 2 or more lines of the body of the letter on the second page BEFORE the closing.
4. The *second page requires a heading,* which is *typed on line 7.* There are two methods appropriate for personal business letters as follows:

METHOD 1

- Type the first line of the inside address at the left margin.
- Type the page number at the center of the page.
- Type the date so that it ends at the right margin.
- Return 3 times after the heading to continue the body of the letter.

METHOD 2

- Type the first line of the inside address at the left margin.
- Return once and type the word "Page" and number at the left margin.
- Return once and type the date at left margin.
- Return 3 times after the heading to continue the body of the letter.

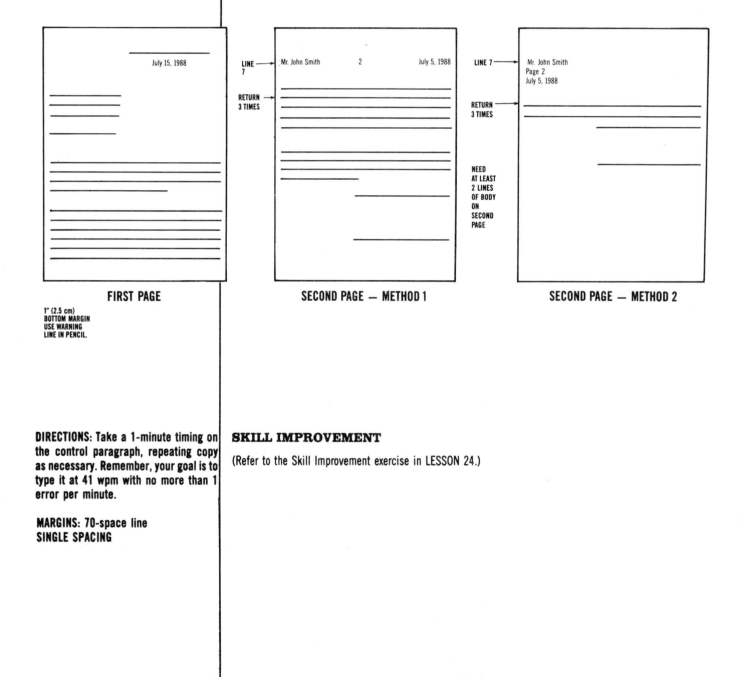

FIRST PAGE

1" (2.5 cm)
**BOTTOM MARGIN
USE WARNING
LINE IN PENCIL.**

SECOND PAGE — METHOD 1

SECOND PAGE — METHOD 2

DIRECTIONS: Take a 1-minute timing on the control paragraph, repeating copy as necessary. Remember, your goal is to type it at 41 wpm with no more than 1 error per minute.

**MARGINS: 70-space line
SINGLE SPACING**

SKILL IMPROVEMENT

(Refer to the Skill Improvement exercise in LESSON 24.)

LESSON 35

OBJECTIVE: To learn how to set up simple tabulations.

DIRECTIONS: Type the warm-up line 3 times with <u>control</u> as your goal.

MARGINS: 60-space line

CENTERING A SIMPLE TABULATION

GOAL: To type 35 or more wpm with no more than 1 error per minute.

ALIGN NUMBERS AT THE RIGHT.

WARM-UP

Have you ever wondered why people do not listen to you?

A tabulation is a synopsis of information arranged in the form of a table.

Procedure for Centering a Simple Tabulation

- Clear all margin stops and all old tabs.
- To center a tabulation problem *horizontally*, we must first determine how many spaces will be left between columns: generally, 6, 8, or 10. The figure chosen depends on the number of columns to be typed and the longest item in each column.
- Next, backspace center the KEY LINE. The key line is made up of the longest item in each column PLUS the number of spaces between columns.
- Set the left margin stop at the point you have completed the backspacing of the key line. The first column will start here.
- To set tab stops for the other columns, use the key line again. Space across once for each stroke in the longest item of a column PLUS the number of spaces between columns, and set a tab for each column.
- To center the tabulation *vertically*, follow the directions in LESSON 33.
- On electronic typewriters, centering tabulations can be done automatically. Check your machine manual to learn the method used.

For practice, set up the following example as you read the directions.

EXAMPLE:
1. Clear margins and tab stops.
2. On elite typewriters, set the left margin at 27 for the first column and a tab stop at 61 for the second column. (On pica machines, the settings are 27 and 44.)
3. Using a half sheet of paper, space down to line 7 from the top edge of the paper.
4. Type the following items, using the tab key for the second column.

(27 spaces)	tabulation	(6 spaces)	heading	(27 spaces)
	centering		column heading	
	intercolumn		subheading	

elite	27	61
pica	27	44

> *NOTE:* In this example, there are 27 spaces at the left margin and a similar number of spaces after the longest line in the second column.

A 3-column table differs from a 2-column table in that there are 2 tab stops. Follow the procedure in the next example to set up a 3-column table:

EXAMPLE:
1. Clear margins and all tab stops.
2. Set the left margin at 18 and tab stops at 44 (elite) or 35 (pica) and at 72 (elite) and 55 (pica).

44-1

DIRECTIONS: The following letter is typed in blocked style with open punctuation. The return address and date appear in the heading beginning on line 15 at the center. Follow this letter line for line, using the instruction information to the left of the letter. When it is completed, proofread it and circle your errors. **SAVE THE LETTER:** It will be used when you learn to type envelopes and practice inserting letters into the envelopes.

MARGINS: 55-space line
SINGLE SPACING

GENERAL:
Set a 55-space line. Use single spacing. Set a tab at center of paper.

HEADING:
Begin on line 15. Start at tab.

Return 5 times. →

INSIDE ADDRESS:

Double-space. →
SALUTATION:
Double-space. →
BODY BEGINS:

Use single spacing. Double-space between paragraphs.

Most good business letters have 3 paragraphs: opening, middle, and closing.

BODY ENDS:
Double-space. →
COMPLIMENTARY CLOSE:
Start at tab. Return 4 times. →

SIGNATURE:
Start at tab. Type your name. Then sign the letter.

2309 Maxwell Avenue
Philadelphia, PA 19115
March 4, 19--

Computer Equipment Corporation
1900 Fifth Avenue
New York, NY 10021

Gentlemen

Will you please send your recent catalog on computers and other equipment being used today in the data processing field.

Our class has been assigned to do a report on "Advances in the Data Processing Field," and I would like to have some pictorial information to be used in addition to my written report. There is always so much progress in this area that it is hard to know what is new and what is old.

Whatever information that you send will be appreciated. I want to do the best job possible for this report as I am considering a career in this field.

Yours very truly

Robin Johnson

(Ms.) Robin Johnson

3. Using a half sheet of paper, space down to line 7 from the top edge of the paper.

4. Type the problem, using the tab key for the second and third columns.

```
tabulation        heading           key line
centering         subheading        back-center
intercolumn       column heading    inspace
```

elite	18	44	72
pica	18	35	55

NOTE: In this example, there are 18 spaces at both the left and right margins, with 6 spaces between columns.

35-1

DIRECTIONS: On a half sheet of paper, type the following information in tabular form, using double spacing and centering the problem both horizontally and vertically. Leave 6 spaces between columns.

NOTICE that numbers (as in Problem 35-1) are aligned at the RIGHT.

To help you get started, the KEY LINE for this problem, using the longest line in each column, would be:

Charlottesville......100......71
          (6 spaces)   (6 spaces)

VIRGINIA TEMPERATURE RANGES

Roanoke	95	71
Richmond	100	76
Lynchburg	96	69
Charlottesville	91	75
Bristol	96	66
Dulles Airport	100	72

35-2

DIRECTIONS: On a half sheet of paper, type the following information in tabular form using single spacing. Center the problem both vertically and horizontally. Leave 10 spaces between columns.

MOHANSIC BASEBALL CLUB
Report of Membership
June 30, 1988

Yorktown	33 boys	47 girls
Somers	63 boys	23 girls
Cortlandt	40 boys	27 girls
Putnam	45 boys	25 girls

SKILL IMPROVEMENT

DIRECTIONS: Type the accuracy and speed lines 3 times each. Take a 1-minute timing on each line, repeating copy as necessary. Then take a 1-minute timing on the control paragraph with 35 wpm as your goal. Indent the first line 5 spaces.

MARGINS: 60-space line
SINGLE SPACING

Accuracy:
```
My friend may be able to go                 6
along with you within two weeks.           12
```

Speed:
```
All of us would benefit if each             6
one of us tried to help out.               12
```

Control Paragraph:
```
     There are many times in life when it is necessary to be   12
able to get along with other people.  One such time is on an   24
occasion of entering your first job.  You will surely be one   36
step closer to success if you are skillful in this important   48
task.  If you find it difficult getting along with others at   60
work, think of some ways you can improve.  You will be happy   72
you made the effort.                                           76
```

```
| 1 | 2 | 3 | 4 | 5 | 6 | 7 | 8 | 9 | 10 | 11 | 12 |
```

LESSON 44

PERSONAL BUSINESS LETTERS

GOAL: To type 41 or more wpm with no more than 1 error per minute.

YOUR LETTER REPRESENTS YOU!

OBJECTIVE: To learn the proper format for typing personal business letters.

DIRECTIONS: Type the warm-up line 3 times with <u>control</u> as your goal.

MARGINS: 70-space line

WARM-UP

The union members held their meeting in a large
air-conditioned hall.

A few of the reasons you might need to type a personal business letter are:

- To ask for information
- To make reservations at a hotel for a vacation
- To write a covering letter for a resume
- To send a thank-you letter after a job interview

These lessons will give you practice in composing, revising, and retyping such letters. In your work, remember that your continued goal should be NEATNESS AND ACCURACY. You should always try to give a good impression, and that impression begins with the way you type your letter and envelope.

Here are illustrations of the 3 most commonly used letter formats. Note the names of the parts of the letter, the style and punctuation used, and the rules for typing that follow.

FULL-BLOCKED STYLE

←HEADING→
INSIDE ←ADDRESS→
←SALUTATION→
←BODY→
COMPLIMENTARY ←CLOSE→ ←SIGNATURE→

BLOCKED STYLE OPEN PUNCTUATION

HEADING→
INSIDE ADDRESS→
SALUTATION→
BODY→
COMPLIMENTARY CLOSE→ SIGNATURE→

SEMI-BLOCKED STYLE MIXED PUNCTUATION

Full-Blocked Style
All letter parts begin at left margin.

Blocked Style
Heading and closing begin at center.
All other lines begin at left margin.

Semi-Blocked Style
Heading and closing begin at center.
First line of paragraph is indented.
All other lines begin at left margin.

Open Punctuation
No colon after salutation. No comma after complimentary close.

Mixed Punctuation
A colon follows salutation. A comma follows complimentary close.

LESSON 36

OBJECTIVE: To practice typing tabulations with column headings.

DIRECTIONS: Type the warm-up line 3 times with <u>speed</u> as your goal.

MARGINS: 70-space line

CENTERING TABULATIONS WITH COLUMN HEADINGS

GOAL: To type 36 or more wpm with no more than 1 error per minute.

WARM-UP

You must never be afraid to raise questions when you seek information.

Procedure for Centering a Tabulation with Column Headings

Column headings fall into 3 categories. They may be:

1. The <u>same</u> number of spaces as the <u>longest</u> item in a column

<u>Room</u>
1013
 907
1202
 819

4 spaces in heading
4 spaces in longest item of column
Subtract: 4
$\frac{-4}{0}$

Begin both at the same point.

2. <u>Shorter</u> than the number of spaces in the longest item in a column

———→<u>Name</u>
Women's Sports Club
Boy Scouts
Lions
Planning Committee

 4 spaces in heading
19 spaces in longest item of column
Subtract: 19   Divide 15 by 2:
$\frac{-4}{15}$ Answer—7½
    (drop fraction)

Begin column heading 7 spaces in from tab.

3. <u>Longer</u> than the number of spaces in the longest item in a column

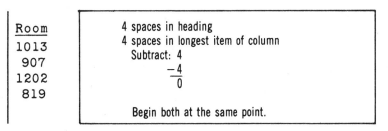

<u>Number</u>
47
32
51
 8

6 spaces in heading
2 spaces in longest item in column
Subtract: 6   Divide 4 by 2:
$\frac{-2}{4}$ Answer—2

Begin column items 2 spaces in from heading tab stop. Change tab from heading to column.

WHEN HORIZONTALLY BACKSPACING a problem, you <u>must</u> use as part of the KEY LINE any column heading that is LONGER than the longest item of a column.

    In preparing a tabulation, once the key line has been backspace centered and the LEFT margin stop and the tabs set, you must determine the relative placement of the column headings to the column or of the column items to the heading. To do this, use the following procedure.

▶ *SEE CATEGORY 1*
    When the column heading is the *same* as the longest item in the column, begin both at the same point.

CHAPTER

VII

PERSONAL BUSINESS LETTERS

► *SEE CATEGORY 2*

When the column heading is *shorter* than the longest item in the column:

A. Count the number of spaces in the column heading.
B. Count the number of spaces in the longest item of the column.
C. Subtract the difference and divide by 2. Drop any fractions.
D. Move in the number of spaces indicated and type the heading.

► *SEE CATEGORY 3*

When the column heading is *longer* than the longest item in the column:

A. Count the number of spaces in the column heading.
B. Count the number of spaces in the longest item of the column.
C. Subtract the difference and divide by 2. Drop any fractions.
D. Move in the number of spaces indicated and type the column items.

NOTE: In this case a TAB STOP was set for the heading when you backspace centered. This tab should be cleared and a NEW TAB set to correspond to the point where the column items will be typed.

EXAMPLE:

For practice, type the following example in tabular form, using a full sheet of paper and double spacing. Center both horizontally and vertically.

MAIN HEADING ——————→
Double-space ↓
SECONDARY HEADING ——————→

Triple-space ↓

COLUMN HEADINGS ——————→
Double-space ↓

BODY OF TABULATION ——————→

ANNUAL CONFERENCE SCHEDULE

Center Hotel

Name	Room	Number
Women's Sports Club	1013	47
Boy Scouts	907	32
Lions	1202	51
Planning Committee	819	8

REMEMBER: The underscore should not undershoot or overshoot the heading.

NOTE: Always double-space. (1 blank line) between the main and secondary headings of the tabulation. Always *triple-space* (2 blank lines) before column headings but *double-space* after.

DIRECTIONS: Type the following tabulation, using a full sheet of paper and double-spacing. Center vertically and horizontally. Leave 6 spaces between columns.

36-1

BIRTHDAYS OF FAMOUS PEOPLE

by Month and Date

Famous Individual	Month	Date
Robert E. Lee	January	19
George Washington	February	22
Abraham Lincoln	February	12
Harry S. Truman	May	8
Pope John Paul II	May	18
John F. Kennedy	May	29

REMEMBER: Are your numbers aligned on the right?

LESSON 43

COMPOSING A PERSONAL BUSINESS NOTE FROM GUIDED SENTENCES

SHOULDERS, ARMS ELBOWS RELAXED?

GOAL: To type 41 or more wpm with no more than 1 error per minute.

OBJECTIVE: To compose a personal business note from facts that are provided.

DIRECTIONS: Type the warm-up line 3 times with <u>accuracy</u> as your goal.

MARGINS: 70-space line

WARM-UP

```
High in the Alps the skiers slid down the hills,
enjoying their sport.
```

NOTE: When composing, you may use DOUBLE SPACING and X-OUT errors. However, remember to return to single spacing and good form when typing the final copy. Use proofreader's marks with red or green pencil for editing before typing good copy.

DIRECTIONS: At the typewriter, on a half sheet of paper, compose a short personal business note using the following guided sentences. Use the blocked style. Refer to LESSON 25 for good ideas for composing. Then remove the rough draft from the typewriter and edit the copy, making additions, deletions, and changes in either pen or pencil. Refer to the method in LESSON 26 and use the proofreaders' symbols in LESSON 24. When your corrections are all made, retype the note in good form from the edited copy. Proofread carefully and make all necessary corrections.

MARGINS: 60-space line
DOUBLE SPACING (rough draft)
SINGLE SPACING (final copy)

43-1

The guided sentences for this personal note are as follows:

1. You have just learned that your friend, John, has received an award for good sportsmanship. You wish to congratulate him for this achievement.

2. Tell him that you realize it must have taken a lot of hard work and perseverance to be considered for such recognition.

3. Mention how proud his family, friends, and schoolmates are. Tell him why you feel particularly appreciative of the good name he has helped bring to the school. Remind him of why you feel this award will be so important for his personal future.

4. Offer best wishes for continued success and close the note.

DIRECTIONS: Take a 1-minute timing on the control paragraph, repeating copy as necessary. Remember, your goal is to type it at 41 wpm with no more than 1 error per minute.

MARGINS: 70-space line
SINGLE SPACING

SKILL IMPROVEMENT

(Refer to the Skill Improvement exercise in LESSON 23.)

DIRECTIONS: Type the following hand-written information in correct tabular form, using a full sheet of paper and double-spacing. Center both horizontally and vertically.

36-2

Beautiful City Parks

Northern Hemisphere

Name of Park	Location	Rating
St. James	London, England	Good
Luxembourg	Paris, France	Ideal
Tivoli	Copenhagen, Denmark	Fine
Central	New York, U.S.A.	Lovely
Fairmount	Philadelphia, U.S.A.	Lovely

NOTE: When finding the KEY LINE in handwritten copy, what may <u>appear</u> to be the longest item in a column may not be. It is best to count the spaces.

DIRECTIONS: Type the following hand-written information in correct tabular form, using a full sheet of paper and double-spacing. Leave 10 spaces between columns. Center both horizontally and vertically.

36-3

Famous Foods

Name	Country of Origin	When Used
Antipasto	Italy	Appetizer
Baklava	Greece	Dessert
Tempura	Japan	Main dish
Arroz con pollo	Spain	Main dish
Fortune cookie	China	Dessert

DIRECTIONS: Type the accuracy and speed lines 3 times each. Take a 1-minute timing on each line, repeating copy as necessary. Then take a 1-minute timing on the control paragraph with 36 wpm as your goal. Indent the first line 5 spaces.

MARGINS: 70-space line
SINGLE SPACING

SKILL IMPROVEMENT

Accuracy:

If you do your work well, you will	7
have a better chance of succeeding.	14

Speed:

Be sure to mail the postcards which	7
Frank had given to you early today.	14

Control Paragraph:

If you travel frequently on business, you should try to stay in a	14
hotel where you will feel comfortable. There are a number of very ex-	28
cellent hotels in Washington, but I am told they are quite expensive.	42
Once you have made your plans to take a trip, you should investigate a	56
number of different hotels where you might stay. Of course, it is not	70
too much to ask that rooms be quiet and clean. Another factor to con-	84
cern yourself with is the number of restaurants within the hotel. Men	98
who travel frequently want convenience and are not concerned with cost.	112

| 1 | 2 | 3 | 4 | 5 | 6 | 7 | 8 | 9 | 10 | 11 | 12 | 13 | 14 |

DIRECTIONS: Type this note, following the same directions as in Problem 42-1.

MARGINS: 60-space line
SINGLE SPACING

42-2

Dear Laura

Congratulations on your change of jobs. I ran into Jane last week, who told me all about it. You must be very excited about your new responsibilities, not to mention the wonderful raise you received.

Let's meet for dinner soon. Is Thursday of next week at 6 p.m. convenient for you? P.J.'s would be a great place to "toast your new post." Why don't you call me at the office? You can easily reach me any day around 4.

Best wishes.

DIRECTIONS: Type this note, following the same directions as in Problem 42-1.

MARGINS: 60-space line
SINGLE SPACING

42-3

Dear Jim,

It was good to see you at the company get-together. You looked great. Your new position seems to appeal to you. Continued good luck!

We are in the process of looking for someone to serve as a consultant on the marketing of a new paper product. Do you know of anyone offhand whom you would like to recommend?

I'm in the office everyday between 9 and 11:30 a.m. If you can think of someone, please let me know. My number is 555-8746.

Thanks a lot.

DIRECTIONS: Take a 1-minute timing on the control paragraph, repeating copy as necessary. Remember, your goal is to type it at 40 wpm with no more than 1 error per minute.

MARGINS: 70-space line
SINGLE SPACING

SKILL IMPROVEMENT

(Refer to the Skill Improvement exercise in LESSON 22.)

CHAPTER

V

FORM TYPING

LESSON

42

OBJECTIVE: To practice typing personal business notes from unarranged, hand-written copy.

DIRECTIONS: Type the warm-up line 3 times with <u>speed</u> as your goal.

MARGINS: 70-space line

DIRECTIONS: Using a half sheet of paper and keeping the same letter format, type the following handwritten note in good form. You must follow the warning bell. Use the current date and sign your name. Proofread carefully and correct all errors.

MARGINS: 60-space line
SINGLE SPACING

TYPING UNARRANGED AND HANDWRITTEN PERSONAL BUSINESS NOTES

DIVIDE A WORD BETWEEN SYLLABLES.

GOAL: To type 40 or more wpm with no more than 1 error per minute.

WARM-UP

The majestic tower stood high in the sky, giving
its glory to the city.

42-1

Dear Mark

What a surprise to meet you at the checkout counter of B and B's last week. It must be at least two or three years since we last saw each other.

It would really be super to get together, don't you think? There is so much to catch up on about what's been happening, both personally and careerwise. Please feel free to call at my office at any time. The number is 555-2901. Let's not wait another two years before we get a chance to chat.

Do call soon.

Cordially

LESSON 37

OBJECTIVE: To learn how to type on lines and fill in blocks on forms.

DIRECTIONS: Type the warm-up line 3 times with <u>accuracy</u> as your goal.

MARGINS: 70-space line

TYPING ON LINES; FILLING IN BLOCKS

GOAL: To type 37 or more wpm with no more than 1 error per minute.

WARM-UP

Reading will help you to improve your command of
the English language.

Procedure for Typing Information on the Lines of a Form

- Adjust the form to the machine. If the lines on the form are slightly slanted, insert the form in a slanted position into the typewriter so the lines are even with the top edge of the alignment scale.
- The line on which you are to type should be slightly below the alignment portion of the alignment scale.
- Letters should rest slightly above the line so that letters with tails (g, y, and q, for example) do not touch the line:

<u>Roger Y. Smith</u>

- Line spacing on printed forms may not equal the normal line spacing on your machine. Therefore, it may be necessary to use the VARIABLE LINE-SPACER each time you return, to adjust for the difference.

> *NOTE:* Depending upon your typewriter, the VARIABLE LINE-SPACER may be a button on the left cylinder knob or the entire cylinder knob itself. Simply push in the variable line-spacer and turn the cylinder knob up or down to adjust the writing line of the form to the top edge of your alignment scale.

Procedure for Filling in Blocks on Forms

- Use the small letter "x" as a check mark.
- Find the beginning of the block. Depending on your typewriter, use the carriage, the half-space key, or cartridge (ribbon container in front of the typing element on IBM Selectives) to move as close to the center of the block as you can. Remember that blocks on forms may not fit the spacing of your typewriter.
- Use the variable line-spacer to align the lower line of the block slightly below the alignment portion of the alignment scale so that letters or numbers will rest slightly above the line as shown in the following example:

YES [x] [ ] Social Security Number [0][0][0] [0][0] [0][0][0]

37-1

DIRECTIONS: Remove the bottom half of Worksheet 1 and insert it into the typewriter. Set your left margin 2 spaces from the left edge of each group of lines. Copy the material exactly as you see it.

LEFT MARGIN ↓

John P. Smith
4618 West Olive Street
San Francisco, CA 94115

LEFT MARGIN ↓

The Alvin Company
Attention: Personnel Dept.
2740 Market Street
Philadelphia, PA 19150

DIRECTIONS: On a half sheet of paper, make a copy of this short personal business note, following the method shown in the sample letter. Note that mixed punctuation is used. Type the current date and sign your name at the end of the note.

MARGINS: 60-space line
SINGLE SPACING

(Date)

Dear John:

What a shame that I did not reach you before you
left for lunch today! I had hoped that we would
get an opportunity to talk about the new sales
policy that is being planned for the coming spring.

Perhaps we can find time to meet at the beginning
of next week. If that is convenient for you,
please let me know as soon as possible.

I look forward to hearing from you.

Cordially,

41-3

DIRECTIONS: On a half sheet of paper, make a copy of the following short personal business note, following the procedure outlined. Use the current date and sign your name at the end of the note.

MARGINS: 60-space line
SINGLE SPACING

(Date)

Dear Cynthia

This is just a note of good wishes before you
leave for your trip to the Continent. You are
going to love Europe. Paris and London are very
exciting cities, the scenery and mountains of
Switzerland and Austria are superb, and the people
of Italy are warm and friendly.

If you get a chance, let me know how you are doing
somewhere halfway through the trip. I would be
interested to know some of your impressions of the
sights you see.

In the meantime, have a great trip.

Sincerely

DIRECTIONS: Take a 1-minute timing on the control paragraph, repeating copy as necessary. Remember, your goal is to type it at 40 wpm with no more than 1 error per minute.

MARGINS: 70-space line
SINGLE SPACING

SKILL IMPROVEMENT

(Refer to the Skill Improvement exercise in LESSON 21.)

DIRECTIONS: Remove the top half of Worksheet 1 and insert it into the typewriter. Then fill in the information given on the following form.

37-2

Richard C. Lowell   Washington High School
Sophomore   Business Education Department
                           14 East River Street
                           Little Falls, NY 12230

Presently Employed   [X]   [ ]
                     Yes   No

Today's   Your
Date   [ ][ ][ ][ ][ ]   Social
                                     Security   [1][7][9][2][0][5][6][2][2]
                                     Number

DIRECTIONS: Type the accuracy and speed lines 3 times each. Take a 1-minute timing on each line, repeating copy as necessary. Then take a 1-minute timing on the control paragraph with 37 wpm as your goal. Indent the first line 5 spaces.

MARGINS: 70-space line
SINGLE SPACING

SKILL IMPROVEMENT

Accuracy:

The thief was very quick to admit	7
that he had stolen the valuable gem.	14

Speed:

A religious person may exhibit a	7
deep sense of feeling for all people.	14

Control Paragraph:

When you must handle more things than you can manage easily, your	14
best course of action is to ask for additional help. To neglect to do	28
so will indicate that you are not a good manager of your time. No one	42
in this world can get along without help from others at various times.	56
Do not think that asking for help will make you a lesser person in the	70
eyes of others. Perhaps just the opposite is true.	80

| 1 | 2 | 3 | 4 | 5 | 6 | 7 | 8 | 9 | 10 | 11 | 12 | 13 | 14 |

LESSON 41

OBJECTIVE: To learn how to type a short personal business note.

DIRECTIONS: Type the warm-up line 3 times with <u>control</u> as your goal.

MARGINS: 70-space line

DIRECTIONS: Using a half sheet of paper, make a copy of the sample personal business note. Follow the procedure given at the left of the note. Use the current date and sign your own name.

MARGINS: 60-space line
SINGLE SPACING

DATE: Start on line 7.   →

     Return 4 times.   →

SALUTATION:
     Return 2 times.   →
BODY BEGINS:

     Use single
     spacing.

     Double-space   →
     between
     paragraphs.

BODY ENDS:
     Return 2 times.   →
COMPLIMENTARY CLOSE:

SIGNATURE:

TYPING ARRANGED PERSONAL BUSINESS NOTES

GOAL: To type 40 or more wpm with no more than 1 error per minute.

WARM-UP

Be aware of the fact that learning to type is one
good skill to master.

To type a short personal business note, use a half-sheet of regular 8½ x 11 paper. The three most commonly used letter formats are explained in detail in LESSON 44: full-blocked style, blocked style, and modified blocked style; open or mixed punctuation. In the sample note in Problem 41-1, the full-blocked style is shown, with open punctuation (no punctuation after the salutation or complimentary close).

41-1

January 5, 19--

Dear Mary

It was good to hear that you have been selected
as editor in chief of your department. Without
question you were the perfect choice. We are sure
you will be successful in your new position and
that you will do a fine job.

Please keep in touch and let us know if we can
help you in any way. We are always pleased and
interested to learn of your progress and advancement.

Sincerely

Bill

LESSON 38

ALIGNING FORM HEADINGS

GOAL: To type 38 or more wpm with no more than 1 error per minute.

OBJECTIVE: To practice aligning headings on forms you may be required to type.

DIRECTIONS: Type the warm-up line 3 times with <u>control</u> as your goal.

MARGINS: 70-space line

WARM-UP

Whenever you speak, do so slowly, using a clear, well-modulated voice.

Procedure for Aligning Form Headings

● Align the bottom edge of the heading words with your alignment scale.
● For clarity, begin typing about 2 or 3 spaces after the heading word, or after the colon that follows the heading word, as shown in the following example:

```
DATE:   Present                 TO:   Juan Diaz
PHONE NUMBER:   555-1212
FROM:   L. Peterson             FROM:   Jean Duval
```

● If a line follows a heading word, align your typewriter with both the heading word and the line (refer to LESSON 37). Begin typing on the line approximately 2 spaces from the end of the heading word.

```
Name:   Alice R. Evanston _____

Name:   Evanston      Alice      R. _____
        LAST          FIRST      MIDDLE INITIAL
```

DIRECTIONS: Remove the bottom part of Worksheet 2 and insert it into the typewriter. Then fill in the information from the following form.

38-1

Name: *Alice R. Evanston*   Date: *January 5, 19__*

Address: *28 Ocean View*   Phone No.: *555-2509*

City, State, Zip: *Atlantic City, NJ 08402*

Registration Desired for: Day [X] Evening [ ]

Referred by: *Employment Division*

CHAPTER

VI

PERSONAL
BUSINESS
NOTES

DIRECTIONS: Type the accuracy and speed lines 3 times each. Take a 1-minute timing on each line, repeating copy as necessary. Then take a 1-minute timing on the control paragraph with 38 wpm as your goal. Indent the first line 5 spaces.

MARGINS: 70-space line
SINGLE SPACING

SKILL IMPROVEMENT

Accuracy:

Your beginning job happens to be	7
where a ladder of success will begin.	14

Speed:

The boys may fix their old car and	7
try to drag race with it on Sunday.	14

Control Paragraph:

Vacation time is probably the high point of the year to most work-	14
ing American families. Plans are generally made for a week or more for	28
this pleasant break from routine. The children do not realize how much	42
in advance it is necessary to plan. First, there must be enough money	56
set aside for vacation. Second, family members must think of the kinds	70
of clothes they must take along. Third, the entire family should be in	84
on planning where the vacation will be spent.	93

| 1 | 2 | 3 | 4 | 5 | 6 | 7 | 8 | 9 | 10 | 11 | 12 | 13 | 14 |

DIRECTIONS: Type the accuracy and speed lines 3 times each. Take a 1-minute timing on each line, repeating copy as necessary. Then take a 1-minute timing on the control paragraph with 40 wpm as your goal. Indent the first line 5 spaces.

MARGINS: 70-space line
SINGLE SPACING

SKILL IMPROVEMENT

Accuracy:

When she sells her business she will	7
have a lot of cash for investment.	14

Speed:

In the next decade there will be a	7
great many secretarial jobs offered.	14

Control Paragraph:

Do you realize that the paper used to print our paper money is no	14
doubt the most precise product in the entire paper industry? Not only	28
does the paper have to be very durable so that it is nearly impossible	42
to tear, but it must weigh a certain amount, it must be of the correct	56
size, and it has to be of such high quality that it cannot possibly be	70
duplicated. If you ever get to Washington, you should make it a point	84
to visit the Bureau of Engraving and Printing. It would highlight any	98
trip to our nation's capital.	104

| 1 | 2 | 3 | 4 | 5 | 6 | 7 | 8 | 9 | 10 | 11 | 12 | 13 | 14 |

LESSON 39

OBJECTIVE: To practice typing various kinds of forms, including an application form.

DIRECTIONS: Type the warm-up line **3** times with <u>speed</u> as your goal.

MARGINS: 70-space line

ALIGNING ITEMS IN COLUMNS; FILLING IN AN APPLICATION FORM

STRIVE FOR ACCURACY!

GOAL: To type 39 or more wpm with no more than 1 error per minute.

WARM-UP

Speeding on the highway, especially if you drink, will cause accidents.

Procedure for Aligning Items in Columns

1. Set a left margin about 2 spaces from the left edge blocking line.
2. For each column, set a tab about 2 spaces to the right of the column line.
3. Type across: type; tab; type; tab; type; return; etc.
4. Adjust the form paper to the machine. Use the variable line-spacer and the alignment scale for each return as the following illustrates:

LEFT MARGIN →   TAB ↓   TAB ↓

Name of School	Dates	Area of Study
P. S. 115	1970–1976	
Central High School	1976–1980	Diploma
Michigan State University	1980–1984	B.A. in History (Ancient)

Typing on Lines with Captions Beneath

Begin typing where the captions start, as the following illustration shows:

Name: Finley   Richard   P.
         <u>LAST</u>   <u>FIRST</u>   <u>MIDDLE INITIAL</u>

DIRECTIONS: Use your typewriter to fill in the personal information asked for.

39-1

(Use the blank form at Worksheet 2.)

LESSON 40

OBJECTIVE: To practice filling in a sample business form.

DIRECTIONS: Type the warm-up line 3 times with <u>accuracy</u> as your goal.

MARGINS: 70-space line

DIRECTIONS: Detach the blank Check Service Application Form on Worksheet 4 and insert it into the typewriter. Type into the appropriate blanks of the form the following information. Make all corrections needed.

FILLING IN A BUSINESS FORM

GOAL: To type 40 or more wpm with no more than 1 error per minute.

WARM-UP

If you ever accuse a man of stealing, be sure your facts are accurate.

40-1

Name: Michael P. Draves
Address: 55 Rural Road
Apt. No.:   2-B
City: Minneapolis
State: MN   *Zip:*   55431

Social Security Number: 999-00-1234

Have you ever had an account with this bank before?   Check "No"
                                                        Leave blank "Savings/Checking"

Name of bank where you have a Savings Account: New York First   *Number:*   32-14771

Name of bank where you have a Checking Account: Type two hyphens (--) in the middle
                                                     of the first answer blank and after "Number."

Previous Employers	Dates	Position
Martin Beck & Company	1973 to 1975	Clerk-typist
World Trade, Inc.	1975 to 1980	Office assistant

Present Employer: The Bowers Company
Date Employed: December, 1980
Address: 3 Union Plaza
City: Minneapolis
State: MN   *Zip:*   55430

Office Phone Number: (612) 555-1212
Position Title: Administrative Asst.

Name of Immediate Supervisor: Paul S. Stern
Title: Office Manager

Personal Reference: Arnold Smith, 10 Tree Street, Minneapolis, MN 55428
Phone No.:   (612) 555-3333

Date: Use current date

Signature: Leave blank

DIRECTIONS: Remove the application form on Worksheet 3 and insert it into your typewriter. Copy the information from the following form. Use correct typing procedure.

APPLICATION FOR EMPLOYMENT

Name *Lowber*   *Robin*   *N.*
      LAST   FIRST   MIDDLE INITIAL

Address *601 East 58 Street*

City *New York*   State *NY*   Zip *10019*   Apt. No. *2B*

Phone No. *(212) 555-3807*   Social Security Number | 8 | 0 | 7 | 3 | 2 | 1 | 0 | 9 | 9 |

Today's Date | | | | | | | Position Desired *Clerk typist*

EDUCATION—LIST IN ORDER:

	Name of School	Location	Dates	Degree
High School	*Washington High School*	*New York City*	*1969-1972*	*Diploma*
College	*Ace Business School*	*New York City*	*1972-1974*	*Certificate*
Other				

EXPERIENCE—LIST MOST RECENT FIRST:

Dates	Name of Company	Location	Salary	Reason for Leaving
7/74-9/76	*B B Mfg. Corporation*	*2 Hall Street New York City*	*$150/wk.*	*Better salary*
9/76-8/79	*The Jayson Company*	*1501 Fifth Avenue New York City*	*$205/wk.*	*Advancement*

Military service: Yes ☐ No ☒   Branch — —

What is your general condition? *Excellent*

Why do you wish to work for this company? *Fine reputation and good career opportunity for advancement*

REFERENCES:

Name	Title	Address
Mr. A. R. Allen	*President*	*B B Mfg. Corporation*
Mrs. T. L. Paul	*Supervisor*	*The Jayson Company*
Ms. Alice Stevens	*Teacher*	*Washington High School New York City*

DIRECTIONS: Type the accuracy and speed lines 3 times each. Take a 1-minute timing on each line, repeating copy as necessary. Then take a 1-minute timing on the control paragraph with 39 wpm as your goal. Indent the first line 5 spaces.

MARGINS: 70-space line
SINGLE SPACING

SKILL IMPROVEMENT

Accuracy:

You might like to work in the office	7
of the president of the corporation.	14

Speed:

Watching people in a bus station in a	7
large city can be quite interesting.	14

Control Paragraph:

One of the most pleasant vacations our family took a year ago was	14
hiking on the many historical trails in our part of Maine. In fact it	28
happened this vacation was the first we had ever gone camping. It was	42
a delightful experience, though I must admit I had misgivings about it	56
as we were planning it. One thing we did learn during this week was a	70
way we could cook in the rain. In fact, we learned enough about it to	84
decide not to do it again. We are going to rent a trailer next year.	98

| 1 | 2 | 3 | 4 | 5 | 6 | 7 | 8 | 9 | 10 | 11 | 12 | 13 | 14 |

USE THIS FORM WITH PROBLEM 37-2:

_____   _____

_____   _____

_____

_____

Presently Employed   ☐   ☐

                   Yes   No

Your
Social
Security
Today's   ☐☐☐☐☐ **Number** ☐☐☐☐☐☐☐☐☐
Date

USE THIS FORM WITH PROBLEM 37-1:

_____   _____

_____   _____

_____   _____

                                                    _____

USE THIS FORM WITH PROBLEM 39-1:

Name: _____
                    LAST   FIRST   MIDDLE INITIAL

Address: _____ Apt. No. _____

City, State, Zip: _____

Phone Number: _____   Today's Date ⬚⬚ ⬚⬚ ⬚⬚

Position Desired: _____   Social
                                          Security   ⬚⬚⬚ ⬚⬚ ⬚⬚⬚⬚
                 _____   Number:

Previous Education:

Name of School	Dates	Area of Study

USE THIS FORM WITH PROBLEM 38-1:

Name: Date:

Address: Phone No.:

City, State, Zip:

Registration Desired for: Day ☐ Evening ☐

Referred by: _____

WORKSHEET 2

USE THIS FORM WITH PROBLEM 39-2:

APPLICATION FOR EMPLOYMENT

Name _____
          LAST   FIRST   MIDDLE INITIAL

Address _____

City _____ State _____ Zip _____ Apt. No. _____

Phone No. _____

Social Security Number ☐☐☐ ☐☐ ☐☐☐☐

Today's Date ☐☐☐☐☐

Position Desired _____

	Name of School	Location	Dates	Degree
EDUCATION—LIST IN ORDER:				
High School				
College				
Other				

Dates	Name of Company	Location	Salary	Reason for Leaving
EXPERIENCE—LIST MOST RECENT FIRST:				

Military service: Yes ☐   No ☐   Branch: _____

What is your general condition? _____

Why do you wish to work for this company? _____

_____

REFERENCES:		
Name	Title	Address

TEAR OFF

- -

USE THIS FORM WITH PROBLEM 40-1:

CHECK SERVICE APPLICATION FORM

Name _____

Address _____ Apt. No. _____

City _____ State _____ Zip _____

Social Security Number ☐☐☐ ☐☐ ☐☐☐☐

Savings ☐
Checking ☐

Have you ever had an account with this bank before? Yes ☐ No ☐

Name of bank where you have a Savings Account? _____ Number _____

Name of bank where you have a Checking Account? _____ Number _____

Previous Employers (Name)	Dates	Position

Present Employer (Name) _____ Date Employed _____

Address _____ City _____ State _____ Zip _____

Office Phone Number _____ Position Title _____

Name of Immediate Supervisor _____ Title _____

Personal Reference:

Name	Address	Phone No.

_____   _____
Date   Signature

WORKSHEET 4

USE THIS FORM WITH PROBLEM 60-3:

Name and Address: Phone:

EDUCATION:

SPECIAL ACCOMPLISHMENTS:

WORK EXPERIENCE:

OTHER INTERESTS:

REFERENCES: